# Uncover 3
Combo B

**Ben Goldstein • Ceri Jones**
with Susan Banman Sileci

## Student's Book

# CAMBRIDGE
## UNIVERSITY PRESS

University Printing House, Cambridge CB2 8BS, United Kingdom

One Liberty Plaza, 20th Floor, New York, NY 10006, USA

477 Williamstown Road, Port Melbourne, VIC 3207, Australia

314–321, 3rd Floor, Plot 3, Splendor Forum, Jasola District Centre, New Delhi – 110025, India

79 Anson Road, #06–04/06, Singapore 079906

Cambridge University Press is part of the University of Cambridge.

It furthers the University's mission by disseminating knowledge in the pursuit of education, learning and research at the highest international levels of excellence.

www.cambridge.org
Information on this title: www.cambridge.org/9781107515116

© Cambridge University Press 2015

This publication is in copyright. Subject to statutory exception and to the provisions of relevant collective licensing agreements, no reproduction of any part may take place without the written permission of Cambridge University Press.

First published 2015

20  19  18  17  16  15  14  13  12  11  10  9  8

Printed in Great Britain by CPI Group (UK) Ltd, Croydon CR0 4YY

*A catalog record for this publication is available from the British Library*

ISBN  978-1-107-49340-7  Student's Book 3
ISBN  978-1-107-49342-1  Student's Book with Online Workbook and Online Practice 3
ISBN  978-1-107-51508-6  Combo 3A
ISBN  978-1-107-51511-6  Combo 3B
ISBN  978-1-107-49347-6  Teacher's Book 3
ISBN  978-1-107-49345-2  Workbook with Online Practice 3
ISBN  978-1-107-49352-0  Presentation Plus Disc 3
ISBN  978-1-107-49348-3  Class Audio CDs (3) 3
ISBN  978-1-107-49350-6  Video DVD 3

Additional resources for this publication at www.cambridge.org/uncover

The publishers have no responsibility for the persistence or accuracy of URLs for external or third-party Internet websites referred to in this publication, and do not guarantee that any content on such websites is, or will remain, accurate or appropriate. Information regarding prices, travel timetables, and other factual information given in this work is correct at the time of first printing but the publishers do not guarantee the accuracy of such information thereafter.

Art direction, book design, photo research, and layout services: QBS Learning
Audio production: John Marshall Media

# Acknowledgments

Many teachers, coordinators, and educators shared their opinions, their ideas, and their experience to help create Uncover. The authors and publisher would like to thank the following people and their schools for their help in shaping the series.

In Mexico:

María Nieves Maldonado Ortiz (Colegio Enrique Rébsamen); Héctor Guzmán Pineda (Liceo Europeo); Alfredo Salas López (Campus Universitario Siglo XXI); Rosalba Millán Martínez (IIPAC [Instituto Torres Quintero A.C.]); Alejandra Rubí Reyes Badillo (ISAS [Instituto San Angel del Sur]); José Enrique Gutiérrez Escalante (Centro Escolar Zama); Gabriela Juárez Hernández (Instituto de Estudios Básicos Amado Nervo); Patricia Morelos Alonso (Instituto Cultural Ingles, S.C.); Martha Patricia Arzate Fernández, (Colegio Valladolid); Teresa González, Eva Marina Sánchez Vega (Colegio Salesiano); María Dolores León Ramírez de Arellano, (Liceo Emperadores Aztecas); Esperanza Medina Cruz (Centro Educativo Francisco Larroyo); Nubia Nelly Martínez García (Salesiano Domingo Savio); Diana Gabriela González Benítez (Colegio Ghandi); Juan Carlos Luna Olmedo (Centro Escolar Zama); Dulce María Pascual Granados (Esc. Juan Palomo Martínez); Roberto González, Fernanda Audirac (Real Life English Center); Rocio Licea (Escuela Fundación Mier y Pesado); Diana Pombo (Great Union Institute); Jacobo Cortés Vázquez (Instituto María P. de Alvarado); Michael John Pryor (Colegio Salesiano Anáhuac Chapalita)

In Brazil:

Renata Condi de Souza (Colégio Rio Branco); Sônia Maria Bernal Leites (Colégio Rio Branco); Élcio Souza (Centro Universitário Anhaguera de São Paulo); Patricia Helena Nero (Private teacher); Célia Elisa Alves de Magalhães (Colégio Cruzeiro-Jacarepaguá); Lilia Beatriz Freitas Gussem (Escola Parque-Gávea); Sandra Maki Kuchiki (Easy Way Idiomas); Lucia Maria Abrão Pereira Lima (Colégio Santa Cruz-São Paulo); Deborah de Castro Ferroz de Lima Pinto (Mundinho Segmento); Clara Vianna Prado (Private teacher); Ligia Maria Fernandes Diniz (Escola Internacional de Alphaville); Penha Aparecida Gaspar Rodrigues (Colégio Salesiano Santa Teresinha); Silvia Castelan (Colégio Santa Catarina de Sena); Marcelo D'Elia (The Kids Club Guarulhos); Malyina Kazue Ono Leal (Colégio Bandeirantes); Nelma de Mattos Santana Alves (Private teacher); Mariana Martins Machado (Britannia Cultural); Lilian Bluvol Vaisman (Curso Oxford); Marcelle Belfort Duarte (Cultura Inglesa-Duque de Caxias); Paulo Dantas (Britannia International English); Anauã Carmo Vilhena (York Language Institute); Michele Amorim Estellita (Lemec – Lassance Modern English Course); Aida Setton (Colégio Uirapuru); Maria Lucia Zaorob (CEL-LEP); Marisa Veiga Lobato (Interlíngua Idiomas); Maria Virgínia Lebrón (Independent consultant ); Maria Luiza Carmo (Colégio Guilherme Dumont Villares/CEL-LEP); Lucia Lima (Independent consultant); Malyina Kazue Ono Leal (Colégio Bandeirantes); Debora Schisler (Seven Idiomas); Helena Nagano (Cultura Inglesa); Alessandra de Campos (Alumni); Maria Lúcia Sciamarelli (Colégio Divina Providência); Catarina Kruppa (Cultura Inglesa); Roberto Costa (Freelance teacher/consultant); Patricia McKay Aronis (CEL-LEP); Claudia Beatriz Cavalieri (By the World Idiomas); Sérgio Lima (Vermont English School); Rita Miranda (IBI – [Instituto Batista de Idiomas]); Maria de Fátima Galery (Britain English School); Marlene Almeida (Teacher Trainer Consultant); Flávia Samarane (Colégio Logosófico); Maria Tereza Vianna (Greenwich Schools); Daniele Brauer (Cultura Inglesa/AMS Idiomas); Allessandra Cierno (Colégio Santa Dorotira); Helga Silva Nelken (Greenwich Schools/Colégio Edna Roriz); Regina Marta Bazzoni (Britain English School); Adriano Reis (Greenwich Schools); Vanessa Silva Freire de Andrade (Private teacher); Nilvane Guimarães (Colégio Santo Agostinho)

In Ecuador:

Santiago Proaño (Independent teacher trainer); Tania Abad (UDLA [Universidad de Las Americas]); Rosario Llerena (Colegio Isaac Newton); Paúl Viteri (Colegio Andino); Diego Maldonado (Central University); Verónica Vera (Colegio Tomás Moro); Mónica Sarauz (Colegio San Gabriel); Carolina Flores (Colegio APCH); Boris Cadena, Vinicio Reyes (Colegio Benalcázar); Deigo Ponce (Colegio Gonzaga); Byron Freire (Colegio Nuestra Señora del Rosario)

The authors and publisher would also like to thank the following contributors, script writers and collaborators for their inspired work in creating Uncover:
Anna Whitcher, Janet Gokay, Kathryn O'Dell, Lynne Robertson, Dana Henricks

| Unit | Vocabulary | Grammar | Listening | Conversation (Useful language) |
|---|---|---|---|---|
| **6 Difficult Decisions** pp. 54–63 | ■ School life ■ Expressions with *make* and *do* | ■ Second conditional ■ Second conditional *yes/no* questions ■ Second conditional *Wh-* questions Grammar reference p. 111 | ■ Would you tell the teacher? | ■ Asking for and giving advice |
| **7 Smart Planet** pp. 64–73 | ■ Materials ■ Eco-construction verbs | ■ Simple present passive ■ Infinitives of purpose ■ Simple past passive Grammar reference p. 112 | ■ Tour of a museum EcoHouse | ■ Apologizing |
| **8 Run for Cover!** pp. 74–83 | ■ Natural disasters ■ Survival essentials | ■ Past perfect ■ Past perfect *yes/no* questions ■ Past perfect and simple past Grammar reference p. 113 | ■ Survival story | ■ Explaining a personal problem |
| **9 He Said, She Said** pp. 84–93 | ■ Reporting verbs ■ Communication methods | ■ Quoted speech vs. reported speech ■ Reported questions Grammar reference p. 114 | ■ Short conversations | ■ Comparing different accounts of a story |
| **10 Don't Give Up!** pp. 94–103 | ■ Goals and achievements ■ Emotions related to accomplishments | ■ Reflexive pronouns ■ Reflexive pronouns with *by* ■ Causative *have/get* Grammar reference p. 115 | ■ Challenging situations | ■ Reassuring someone |

Unit 6–10 Review Game pp. 104–105

| Writing | Reading | Video | Accuracy and fluency | Speaking outcomes |
|---|---|---|---|---|
| ■ An article about online safety | ■ *A School with a Difference*<br>■ Reading to write: *How to Be Safe Online!*<br>■ Culture: *Punishment or Rehabilitation?* | ■ *Working Together*<br>■ *Who would you talk to if you needed advice?*<br>■ *Watch Your Identity* | ■ Pronunciation of /ʊ/ and /u/<br>■ Using the simple past after *if* in the second conditional | I can . . .<br>■ talk about school life.<br>■ talk about good and bad behavior at school and home.<br>■ discuss difficult situations.<br>■ ask for and give advice.<br>■ discuss different systems for dealing with crime. |
| ■ A newspaper article about an event | ■ *Houses Made of Garbage*<br>■ Reading to write: *Volunteers Clean Valley Nature Reserve*<br>■ Culture: *Under the Australian Sun* | ■ *Where Does it All Go?*<br>■ *What kind of volunteer work can you do in your school or town?*<br>■ *Build It Better*<br>■ *Driving into the Future* (CLIL Project p. 119) | ■ Including *is* or *are* in passive sentences | I can . . .<br>■ identify materials.<br>■ talk about how people recycle and reuse materials.<br>■ talk about eco-construction.<br>■ apologize.<br>■ discuss solar energy and sun safety. |
| ■ A story about a personal experience | ■ *Krakatoa*<br>■ Reading to write: *Story Source*<br>■ Culture: *It isn't just a hobby.* | ■ *Land of Volcanoes*<br>■ *Do you often lose things?*<br>■ *Storm Chasers* | ■ Pronunciation of /æ/ and /ɒ/<br>■ Using the past perfect for events completed before another past moment | I can . . .<br>■ discuss natural disasters.<br>■ ask and answer questions about past experiences.<br>■ discuss past events.<br>■ ask about and discuss personal problems.<br>■ discuss tornadoes and people who chase tornadoes. |
| ■ An essay about social networking sites | ■ *Communication Changes*<br>■ Reading to write: *Are Cell Phones Good for Teenagers?*<br>■ Culture: *The World Speaks One Language* | ■ *Social Networks*<br>■ *What do you think about celebrity gossip?*<br>■ *The Language of the Future?*<br>■ *Pictures with Meaning* (CLIL Project p. 120) | ■ Pronunciation of final consonants /d/, /l/, /m/, and /n/<br>■ Not using *do* in reported questions | I can . . .<br>■ talk about different ways of speaking.<br>■ discuss social networking.<br>■ talk about different communication methods.<br>■ compare stories.<br>■ discuss language use throughout the world. |
| ■ A personal action plan | ■ *Make Your Dreams Come True*<br>■ Reading to write: *Achieving My Goal*<br>■ Culture: *Olympics for the Brain* | ■ *Lifeguard and Athlete*<br>■ *Have you ever given a class presentation?*<br>■ *Circus Star* | ■ The sound /iː/ in words with the letters *ie* and *ei*<br>■ Consonant clusters<br>■ Getting/having something done | I can . . .<br>■ talk about goals and accomplishments.<br>■ discuss emotions related to accomplishments.<br>■ discuss steps toward achieving goals.<br>■ reassure someone.<br>■ discuss an academic competition. |

**Irregular verbs p. 121**

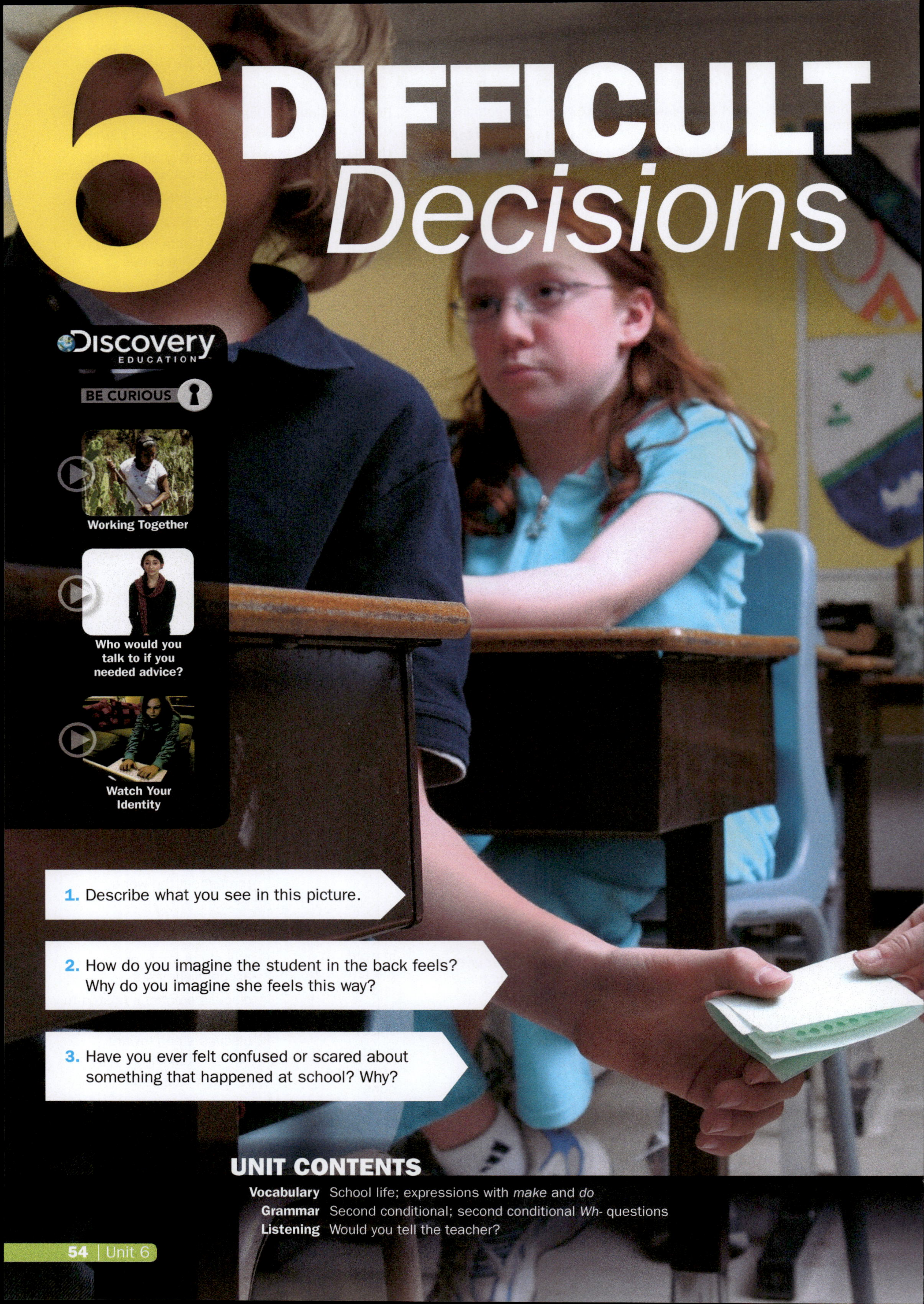

# 6 DIFFICULT Decisions

**Discovery EDUCATION**
BE CURIOUS

Working Together

Who would you talk to if you needed advice?

Watch Your Identity

1. Describe what you see in this picture.

2. How do you imagine the student in the back feels? Why do you imagine she feels this way?

3. Have you ever felt confused or scared about something that happened at school? Why?

## UNIT CONTENTS

**Vocabulary** School life; expressions with *make* and *do*
**Grammar** Second conditional; second conditional *Wh-* questions
**Listening** Would you tell the teacher?

## Vocabulary: School life

**1. Read the phrases related to school life. Then circle the correct answers.**

| being assigned to detention | cheating | wearing a uniform |
| being punctual | following the dress code | winning a prize |
| being rude | getting sent to the principal's office | |
| bullying | getting extra credit | |

1. You can _____ in English if you read two books over the vacation.
   a. get sent to the principal's office    b. get extra credit
2. I'm sorry, but you can't wear those boots to school. You need to _____.
   a. follow the dress code    b. win a prize
3. Emily _____ because she was rude to Mr. Moore.
   a. cheated    b. got sent to the principal's office
4. If you're late to class three times in a semester, you will _____.
   a. wear a uniform    b. be assigned to detention
5. Don't use your cell phone during a test. That's _____.
   a. cheating    b. getting extra credit
6. All students must treat each other with respect. We don't tolerate _____ in our school.
   a. bullying    b. being punctual
7. I think you should join the Math Challenge team. You might _____.
   a. win a prize    b. be rude
8. Mike is never late to class. It's important to him to _____.
   a. follow the dress code    b. be punctual
9. A lot of students don't like _____, but I do. It saves me money on clothes.
   a. wearing a uniform    b. being assigned to detention
10. Christine _____ to the Spanish teacher yesterday. Usually, she's very polite.
    a. was assigned to detention    b. was rude

> **Say it RIGHT!**
> Notice the way these words are pronounced. Then add one more word for each sound.
> /ʊ/ would, could, bullying, _____
> /u/ do, rude, you, _____

 **2. Listen, check, and repeat.**

**3. Put the phrases from Exercise 1 in the correct categories.**

| Rewards | Punishments | Good behavior | Bad behavior |
| --- | --- | --- | --- |
|  |  |  |  |

## Speaking: Actions and consequences

**4. YOUR TURN Work with a partner. Ask and answer the questions.**

1. What rewards and punishments do students get at your school?
2. Do you think your school is strict? Why? / Why not?

> *Teachers sometimes play a game after we've done good work.*

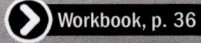 Workbook, p. 36

**Reading** A School with a Difference; How to Be Safe Online!; Punishment or Rehabilitation?
**Conversation** Asking for and giving advice
**Writing** An article about online safety

# YOU make the RULES!

## A SCHOOL WITH A DIFFERENCE

*This week's student reporter, Jodi White, visits the Brooklyn Free School in New York.*

It's Wednesday morning, and it's time for the weekly school meeting. This week's topic is "wheels." One student proposes a new rule that students can bring skateboards, skates, and bicycles to school. A teacher suggests that they do this one day a week, and the whole school votes on a "wheels" day for next Friday. As simple as that! Would I be able to change the rules in my school if I wanted to? No, if I wanted to change the rules, it would be really hard!

But the Brooklyn Free School is different. Here the students make the decisions – about everything! They can decide to go to class or they can decide to watch TV or play a computer game, but most students choose to go to class – it's more interesting! When they don't like a class, they just walk out. If I didn't stay until the end of a class at my school, I'd be assigned to detention!

At the Free School, the teachers don't assign students to detention, and no one gets sent to the principal's office. The students choose what they want to study and how. If you were at the school and you wanted to study car mechanics, for example, or cooking, would the school let you do it? Yes. If you wanted to start a new school magazine, you would suggest it, and together the school would find a way to do it.

That's how the Free School works. The ideas come from the students, and everyone works together to make them happen. I'd love to go to the Free School!

**DID YOU KNOW…?**
There are more than 90 schools like the Brooklyn Free School in the United States. They're sometimes called "anarchistic free schools" or "free skools."

### Reading: An article from a school newspaper

1. Look at the title of the article and the name of the school. What kind of school is it? Why do they describe it as "free"?

2. Read and listen to the article about a school in New York. What are two ways that this school is different from your school?

3. Read the article again. Are these sentences true (*T*) or false (*F*)?

   1. The school has meetings every month. ___
   2. The students make suggestions, and the teachers vote on their suggestions. ___
   3. There are no rules. ___
   4. The students choose their own subjects. ___
   5. The teachers don't tell the students what to do. ___
   6. The reporter doesn't want to study at the Free School. ___

4. **YOUR TURN** Work with a partner. Ask and answer the questions.

   1. Would you like to go to a school like the Brooklyn Free School? Why? / Why not?
   2. How much can students change the rules or classes at your school?
   3. What kinds of classes would you like to take that your school doesn't offer? Where could you learn those things outside of school?

   > I think I'd like that school. If you want, you can watch TV!

   > I'd like it because I could choose what I wanted to study. . . .

# Grammar: Second conditional

**5. Complete the chart.**

| Imaginary situation | Possible consequences |
|---|---|
| *if* + simple past<br>**If** I **changed** the school rules, | *would (not)* + base form of the verb<br>students **wouldn't wear** uniforms. |
| **If** you **missed** class,<br>**If** she **didn't like** the class, | you _____ **be** assigned to detention.<br>she _____ **go**. |

*Many American English speakers use* were *rather than* was *after* I, he, she, *and* it, *especially in a more formal style.*

| Formal style | Informal style |
|---|---|
| If I _____ rude to my teacher, my parents would be very mad at me. | If I _____ always punctual, I wouldn't be assigned to detention so much. |

> Check your answers: Grammar reference, p. 111

**6. Circle the correct answers.**

1. If I **was / would be** rude to a teacher, I **got / would be** assigned to detention.
2. If I **didn't / wouldn't** pass my finals, my parents **didn't / wouldn't** be very happy.
3. If a teacher **sent / would send** me to the principal's office, I **felt / would feel** embarrassed.
4. My teacher **called / would call** my parents if I **didn't / wouldn't** go to school.
5. My friends **did / would like** to go to the Free School if they **opened / would open** one in our town.
6. I **didn't / wouldn't** study math if I **went / would go** to the Free School.

**7. Complete the sentences with the correct form of the verbs.**

1. If I _____ (come) home late one night, . . .
   a. my parents _____ (be) very angry. I _____ (get) some kind of punishment.
   b. my parents _____ (talk) to me about the issue.
   c. my parents _____ (not say) anything.
2. If I _____ (say) something rude to my parents, . . .
   a. I _____ (feel) bad, and I _____ (say) sorry immediately.
   b. they _____ (ask) me what I was upset about.
   c. they _____ (punish) me with no TV or computer for a week.
3. If I _____ (borrow) something from my friend without asking, . . .
   a. it _____ (not be) a problem. My friend does it to me all the time!
   b. my friend probably _____ (not talk) to me for a week!
   c. I _____ (put) it back before they noticed.

> **Second conditional yes/no questions**
>
> Use *if* to ask yes/no questions in the second conditional.
>
> **If** your teacher **got** angry with you in class, **would** you **feel** embarrassed?
>
> **Would** you **say** anything **if** your teacher **forgot** to give you homework?
> Yes, I **would**.
> No, I **wouldn't**.

# Speaking: If I did that, . . .

**8.** YOUR TURN  Circle the answers in Exercise 7 that are true for you. Then compare your answers with a partner.

*If I came home late one night, I'd get some kind of punishment for sure!*

> Workbook, p. 37

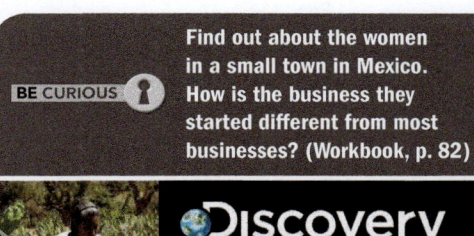

BE CURIOUS — Find out about the women in a small town in Mexico. How is the business they started different from most businesses? (Workbook, p. 82)

**Discovery EDUCATION**

6.1 WORKING TOGETHER

# What would YOU DO?

## Listening: Would you tell the teacher?

1. Work with a partner. What would you do if you saw one of your classmates cheating on a test? What if you found a wallet full of money in the street?

 2. Listen to a conversation between two teenagers, Rachel and Luke. What are they discussing?

 3. Listen again. Circle the correct answers.

1. If Rachel saw a classmate cheating on a test, she would . . .
   a. say nothing and continue with her work.
   b. tell a teacher.
   c. try to cheat as well.

2. If Luke found a wallet full of money on the street near his school, he would . . .
   a. take it to the nearest police station.
   b. give it to a teacher at school.
   c. keep it.

3. If Rachel borrowed something from a friend and then lost it, she would . . .
   a. tell her friend.
   b. buy a new one.
   c. say nothing and hope the friend doesn't notice.

## Vocabulary: Expressions with *make* and *do*

4. Complete the email with *make* or *do*. Then listen and check your answers.

---

**To:** dan@cup.org
**From:** eric@cup.org
**Subject:** Advice

Hi Dan,
I need your advice. We have to give presentations in science class tomorrow, and I have a problem. One of my classmates, Jeremy, asked me to ¹ _do_ **him a favor**: He wanted me to help him with his presentation. Jeremy doesn't like science, and he doesn't like to ² _____ **homework**, but I agreed to help him. We started to ³ _____ **research** together, but he was bored. "Let's hurry up so we can ⁴ _____ **something fun**!" he said. He started to copy whole paragraphs from the Internet and paste them into his presentation. I explained that you can use the Internet for research, but you shouldn't copy like that. "It won't ⁵ _____ **a difference**," he said. "Mrs. Lewis won't find out." Then he looked at my presentation and copied from me! I didn't want to ⁶ _____ **him mad**, so I didn't say anything else. I'm new to this school, and I want to ⁷ _____ **friends**, but I also want to ⁸ _____ **the right thing**. What should I do?
Eric

---

5. **YOUR TURN** Work with a partner. Ask and answer the questions.

1. How often do you do homework with your friends?
2. Is doing homework with someone a good way to make new friends? Why or why not?
3. Eric wants to do the right thing. What do you think he should do in this situation?

## Grammar: Second conditional Wh- questions

**6. Complete the chart.**

*Use Wh- questions in the second conditional to ask about imaginary situations and possible consequences.*

| What | would your teacher do | if | one of your classmates _____ on a test? |
|---|---|---|---|
| Who | would you talk to | if | you _____ a serious problem with a friend? |
| When | would you go to school | if | you _____ the days you went? |
| If | you wanted to do something fun this weekend, | where | would you _____? |
| If | you got a new pet, | why | would you _____ one kind of pet over another? |

> Check your answers: Grammar reference, p. 111

**7. Circle the correct answers.**

1. What **did / would** you do if you **were / would be** the principal at your school?
2. If you **needed / would need** to find a quiet place to study at your school, where **would you go / did you go**?
3. Who would you **do / did** research on if you **have / had** to give a presentation on someone famous?
4. If you **get / got** perfect grades, what would your parents **say / said**?
5. When would you **apologize / apologized** if you **make / made** your best friend mad – at that moment, or a few days later?
6. If you **have / had** to make a difficult decision, who **will / would** you ask to help you?

**8. Complete the conversation.**

A: What ¹_____ you _____ (do) if another kid in your school ²_____ (bully) you?
B: I don't know. Maybe I ³_____ (hide).
A: Really? Where ⁴_____ you _____ (hide)?
B: I don't know. But, hiding isn't a good idea. I know! I ⁵_____ (fight) the bully.
A: Really? Where ⁶_____ you _____ (have) the fight?
B: Maybe outside? But, no. A fight ⁷_____ (be) stupid. I ⁸_____ (talk) to someone about the problem.
A: Who ⁹_____ you _____ (tell)?
B: My parents, probably. Let me ask you a question: Why ¹⁰_____ you _____ (ask) me crazy questions like this?
A: It's for the school newspaper. I'm talking to a lot of people about bullying.

> **Get it RIGHT!**
>
> Use the simple past after *if* with the second conditional.
> If our teacher **gave** extra credit, my grades would be better. NOT: ~~If our teacher **gives** extra credit, my grades would be better.~~

## Speaking: In this situation, I would . . .

**9. YOUR TURN** Work with a partner. Ask and answer the questions.

1. If you were home alone and someone knocked on the door, what would you do?
2. What would you do if you found out your best friend lied to you about lots of things?
3. If you were 18, what would you do that you can't do now?
4. What would you do if you decided to stay home from school one day?

> *If I were home alone and someone knocked on the door, I would make sure I knew the person before I opened the door.*

**REAL TALK** 6.2 WHO WOULD YOU TALK TO IF YOU NEEDED ADVICE?

# I need your ADVICE.

## Conversation: I don't know what to do!

1. **REAL TALK** Watch or listen to the teenagers. Check (✓) the three people that are <u>not</u> mentioned.

   | | | |
   |---|---|---|
   | ☐ aunt | ☐ cousin | ☐ mother |
   | ☐ best friend | ☐ father | ☐ neighbor |
   | ☐ brother | ☐ grandmother | ☐ sister |

2. **YOUR TURN** Who would you talk to if you needed advice? Tell your partner.

3. Listen to Hayley talking to her friend Josh about a problem. Complete the conversation.

   **USEFUL LANGUAGE: Asking for and giving advice**
   
   If I were you    ✓ What's going on?    I need some advice.
   
   Sure. What's up?    What should I do?    Have you tried

   **Hayley:** Josh, can I talk to you?
   **Josh:** Yes, of course. ¹_____What's going on?_____
   **Hayley:** ²_____ I don't know what to do.
   **Josh:** ³_____
   **Hayley:** Well, there's a girl in my class who is saying nasty things about me.
   **Josh:** Really? What sort of things?
   **Hayley:** Oh, that I copy her homework and cheat on tests. It's awful! ⁴_____
   **Josh:** ⁵_____, I wouldn't listen to her. What do your other friends say?
   **Hayley:** They say the same thing. But I can't help it.
   **Josh:** Hmm. ⁶_____ talking to her about it?
   **Hayley:** Yeah, but it doesn't change anything. She keeps doing it.
   **Josh:** Let's talk to her together. Maybe that will help.
   **Hayley:** That's a good idea. Thanks, Josh!

4. Practice the conversation with a partner.

5. **YOUR TURN** Work with a partner. Take turns asking for and giving advice. Use the problems below or your own ideas.

   **Problem 1**
   Someone in your class has taken your backpack. No one knows who took it.

   **Problem 2**
   You can't find some books you left in the classroom yesterday.

# HOW TO BE SAFE ONLINE!

It's easy to bully someone online, and many teenagers suffer from this. So how can you make sure it doesn't happen to you? Follow our essential advice.

> Don't post contact information (address, email, cell phone number) online.
> Check your privacy settings on social networking sites. Make sure you know how to keep your personal information private.
> Don't share your online passwords, not even with your best friends.
> Never respond or retaliate if someone bullies you. This can make things worse.
> You should block any users who send you nasty messages, even if they're your friends.
> Think carefully about posting photos of yourself online. Once your picture is online, anyone can download, share, or even change it.
> Don't ignore cyberbullying or keep it secret. You should ALWAYS tell someone.

## Reading to write: An advice article

**6. Look at the picture and read the article. What is it about?**

> ● *Focus on* **CONTENT**
> When you write an article to help people solve a problem, you can include this information:
> - a title
> - the problem you will give advice about
> - who the problem affects
> - a question that the article will try to answer
> - a list of short, clear pieces of advice

**7. Read the article again. Does it include all of the things from the Focus on Content box? How many pieces of advice are there?**

> ● *Focus on* **LANGUAGE**
> **Giving advice in writing**
> Use the imperative to give advice in writing.
> Affirmative: base form
> **Block** people who are rude to you.
> Negative: *Don't* + base form
> **Don't forget** to check your privacy settings.

**8. Find one other way to give advice in the article.**

**9. Complete the sentences.**

| ✓ Don't | Make | Never | should | think |

1. _Don't_ forward cyberbullying videos or messages about other people.
2. You _____ never give anyone your passwords.
3. If someone bullies you, _____ carefully about changing your user ID and profile.
4. _____ sure you report anything abusive you see online.
5. _____ agree to keep chats with people you don't know "secret."

**Writing:** An advice article

◯ **PLAN**
Think of a problem that you think might affect your classmates, friends, or people in your town. Use the guidelines in the Focus on Content box, and make a list of six pieces of advice you would give to solve the problem.

◯ **WRITE**
Write your article. Use your notes and the online safety article above to help you. Write about 120 words.

◯ **CHECK**
Can you say "yes" to these questions?
- Is the information from the Focus on Content box in your article?
- Have you given advice using the imperative, both affirmative and negative?

Workbook, pp. 40–41

# PUNISHMENT OR REHABILITATION?

**If a teenager committed a crime in your neighborhood, what do you think should happen?**

### The case for punishment:
It's all about consequences. If I didn't study for a test, I wouldn't pass it. If I put my hand in a fire, I would be burned. Simple. So if you commit a crime, you should face the consequences, and that's prison. I heard about a program in Switzerland where teenagers who commit crimes get free school, sports, psychological help, and even a place to live. Are you kidding? That's expensive – more expensive than prison. Our tax money should help society, not people who break the rules of society.
**Ellie, 15, Portland, Maine**

### The case for rehabilitation:
What teenagers need when they're in trouble is help – and we need to spend our tax money to help them. The program in Switzerland was expensive, but it helped teenagers stop committing crimes. Teenagers need to learn that there are alternatives to crime. They need to learn skills so that they can get a job. They need to believe that they are valuable members of society. If you throw them in prison and forget about them, they learn to become better criminals, not better citizens.
**Collin, 16, Boise, Idaho**

**? What should we do with teenagers who commit crimes? Lock them up, or help them change their lives?**

## Culture: Juvenile justice

1. Look at the photo. What do you think society should do with teenagers who commit crimes? Why?

2. **6.08** Read and listen to the debate. How does Ellie answer the question in Exercise 1? How does Collin answer it?

3. Read the debate again. Answer the questions.
    1. According to Ellie, what should the consequences of committing a crime be?
    2. What did the program in Switzerland give teenagers who committed a crime?
    3. How does Ellie think tax money should be spent?
    4. What does Collin think teenagers in trouble need?
    5. What is the purpose of teaching skills to teenagers who commit a crime?
    6. What does Collin believe happens when you put teenagers in prison?

4. **YOUR TURN** Work with a partner. Ask and answer the questions.
    1. Do you agree with Ellie or Collin? Why?
    2. Is there a program in your country like the program in Switzerland? Do you think it's a good idea?
    3. Can you think of one or two solutions to teenage crime that don't involve prison or expensive programs?

**BE CURIOUS** Find out about staying safe online. Who does the video say are the number-one victims of identity theft? (Workbook, p. 83)

**Discovery EDUCATION**
**6.3 WATCH YOUR IDENTITY**

# UNIT 6 REVIEW

## Vocabulary

**1. Match the words with the definitions.**

1. uniform ___
2. detention ___
3. dress code ___
4. punctual ___
5. bullying ___
6. cheating ___

a. on time, not late
b. rules about what clothes to wear
c. copying another student's work
d. special clothes for school
e. a type of punishment
f. being aggressive to another person

## Grammar

**2. Complete the sentences with the second conditional forms of the verbs.**

1. If you _____ (be) more confident, you _____ (make) more friends.
2. If he _____ (not go) to school, he _____ (be) bored.
3. If they _____ (wear) uniforms, they _____ (look) the same.
4. We _____ (have) more free time if we _____ (not have) so much homework.
5. You _____ (not be) so tired if you _____ (not stay) up late.
6. If she _____ (study) harder, she _____ (get) better grades at school.

**3. Write questions using the second conditional.**

1. What / you / do / if / you / see someone cheating on a test?

   _____

2. Where / you live / if / you / can go anywhere in the world?

   _____

3. If / you / win / $5,000 / what / you / do?

   _____

4. If / your friend / not answer / your email / what / you / say?

   _____

5. If / you / not pass / your next test / you / feel upset?

   _____

6. What / you / do / if / you / can live forever?

   _____

## Useful language

**4. Complete the conversation.**

| going on | I were | What should |
|---|---|---|
| Have you | some advice | |

**Bryce:** Hey, Kelly, I really need [1]_____.
**Kelly:** You do? OK. What's [2]_____?
**Bryce:** I was assigned to detention because I've been late for my history class three times this semester.
**Kelly:** That's not so terrible.
**Bryce:** Yes, it is. My parents get really mad about that kind of thing. [3]_____ I do?
**Kelly:** If [4]_____ you, I would be totally honest and tell them the truth.
**Bryce:** No, they never listen. They just get mad and stay mad.
**Kelly:** [5]_____ tried talking to them? You never know.
**Bryce:** That's true. I'm not a little kid anymore. Maybe they'll really listen.
**Kelly:** Give it a try. You never know.

---

**PROGRESS CHECK: Now I can . . .**

☐ talk about school life.
☐ talk about good and bad behavior at school and home.
☐ discuss difficult situations.
☐ ask for and give advice.
☐ write about school rules.
☐ discuss different systems for dealing with crime.

# 7 Smart PLANET

**Discovery EDUCATION**

**BE CURIOUS**

- Where Does It All Go?
- What kind of volunteer work do you do?
- Build It Better
- Driving into the Future

1. Describe what you see in this picture.
2. How does this picture make you feel?
3. Which things in the picture are natural and which are man-made?

## UNIT CONTENTS

**Vocabulary** Materials; eco-construction verbs
**Grammar** Simple present passive; infinitives of purpose; simple past passive
**Listening** Tour of a museum EcoHouse

## Vocabulary: Materials

**1. Match the words with the correct pictures.**

1. _g_  bricks
2. ___ plastic
3. ___ metal
4. ___ glass
5. ___ water
6. ___ cotton
7. ___ paper
8. ___ cement
9. ___ rubber
10. ___ wood
11. ___ plants

 **2. Listen, check, and repeat.**

**3. Write the materials.**

1. We often use this material to make furniture like chairs and tables. _____
2. This material is very common for making T-shirts. _____
3. We make tires for cars with this material. _____
4. We use this material to make books and magazines. _____
5. We usually use this material to make knives, forks, and spoons. _____
6. This material is often gray, and we use it to build bridges and buildings. _____

## Speaking: What's in your house?

**4.** 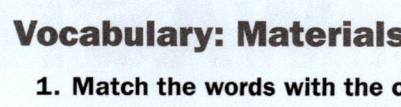 Think about your house or apartment. Write as many objects as you can think of for each material below.

| Cotton | Glass | Wood | Paper | Rubber | Plastic | Metal |
|--------|-------|------|-------|--------|---------|-------|
|        |       |      |       |        |         |       |
|        |       |      |       |        |         |       |
|        |       |      |       |        |         |       |

**5. Work with a partner. Talk about the things in your house.**

*My family has a beautiful glass vase in the living room and . . .*

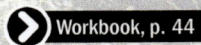 Workbook, p. 44

**Reading** Houses Made of Garbage; Volunteers Clean Valley Nature Reserve; Under the Australian Sun
**Conversation** Apologizing
**Writing** A newspaper article about an event

Unit 7 | **65**

# A WAR Against WASTE

## HOUSES Made of GARBAGE

**Mike Reynolds builds houses from recycled materials.** These houses are a symbol of his war against waste. Mike's houses are built using the things that other people throw away. His Earthships (as his houses are called) are beautiful buildings. They are shaped and colored to reflect the landscape around them. He uses bottles to create beautiful walls full of light. There are plants everywhere, inside and out. But the plants and the bottles, like everything else in the Earthships, are not only there for decoration.

Every single material in an Earthship is carefully chosen. Old car tires are used to build strong external walls. The rubber protects the houses from the cold northern winds in winter. These walls are built at the back of the house. The external walls at the front of the house are built from metal cans or glass bottles, instead of bricks. They're held together with earth from the ground around them. No cement is used at all.

The beautiful bottle walls are built to the south to give light during the day. The larger front windows heat the house. They also create perfect conditions for growing all kinds of fruits and vegetables because the plants are protected against the bad weather. When you live in an Earthship, you don't need anything from the outside world. You grow your own food, you get electricity from the sun and wind, and you get water from the rain and snow.

Mike and the Earthship organization use their ability and experience to help people all over the world. In 2010, they visited victims of the earthquake in Haiti. They taught them how to build safe, new homes quickly and cheaply from materials that they could find around them. Mike points out that trash only exists because we humans create it – but we can also learn to recycle it.

**DID YOU KNOW...?**
Recycled car tires are used to build roads and sidewalks.

## Reading: A magazine article

1. **Look at the picture. Work with a partner. Ask and answer the questions.**
   1. What are the people building?
   2. What materials are they using?
   3. Why are they using them?

2.  **Read and listen to an article about Mike Reynolds. What kind of houses does he build?**

3. **Read the article again. Answer the questions.**
   1. How does Mike protect his Earthships from the cold?
   2. How does he provide light during the day?
   3. Why does he grow his plants in the front of the house?
   4. How does he get energy and water?
   5. How did he and his organization help other people?
   6. What is Mike's main message to the world?

4. **YOUR TURN Work with a partner. Ask and answer the questions.**
   1. Are the materials that Mike Reynolds uses for his Earthships available where you live? What other recycled materials from your area could be used for an Earthship?
   2. Are Earthships practical or possible where you live?
   3. What is your opinion of Earthships? Would you like to live in an Earthship? What would your ideal Earthship look like?

# Grammar: Simple present passive

**5. Complete the chart.**

Use the passive when it is not important who does the action, or when you don't know who does it. To form the simple present passive, use is/are + past participle.

| Active | Passive |
|---|---|
| **Affirmative** ||
| They **make** this wall of bottles. | This wall _____ **made** of bottles. |
| People **use** car tires to build strong walls. | Car tires **are** _____ to build strong walls. |
| **Negative** ||
| They **don't make** that bottle of plastic. | That bottle **isn't** _____ of plastic. |
| People **don't build** the houses with bricks. | The houses _____ **built** with bricks. |

> Check your answers: Grammar reference, p. 112

**6. Complete the sentences with the simple present passive forms of the verbs.**

1. The house ___is made___ (make) of bottles and cans.
2. Rubber tires _____ (not recycle) in some areas.
3. The water from the kitchen _____ (reuse) in the yard.
4. The recycling bins _____ (not clean) every week.
5. A lot of energy _____ (consume) in most houses.
6. This wall _____ (not decorate) with colored bottles.

**7. Write simple present passive sentences. Use infinitives of purpose.**

1. wood / use / build / houses in this neighborhood / .
   ___Wood is used to build houses in this neighborhood.___
2. these plants / grow / provide / people with food / .
   _____
3. walls / design / protect / people from extreme temperatures / .
   _____
4. heat from the sun / use / give / power to the house / .
   _____
5. cans / recycle / create / walls / .
   _____

**Infinitives of purpose**

Use infinitives of purpose to say why something is done.

I recycle my bottles **to help the environment**.

Plants are used **to prevent flooding**.

# Speaking: Plan a building!

**8. YOUR TURN** Work with a partner. Plan a new building that is made from recycled materials. What can you do with the materials below? Write your ideas and add other materials and uses. Be creative!

| Glass bottles | Car or bike tires | Newspapers | Soda cans | Old clothes |
|---|---|---|---|---|
| beautiful chandeliers | | | | |

**9. Join another pair. Tell them about your new building.**

> In our building, glass bottles are used to make beautiful chandeliers and lamps.

> And newspapers are used . . .

**BE CURIOUS** Find out about the trash in our oceans. How many kilos of trash do we throw in the oceans every day? (Workbook, p. 84)

7.1 WHERE DOES IT ALL GO?

# New Challenges, NEW SOLUTIONS

### Listening: Tour of a museum EcoHouse

1. Look at the picture. How is the room similar to and different from the living room in your home?

2. Listen to a guide explaining the living room. It's part of an exhibit. What kind of living room is it?
   a. A historical living room
   b. A living room of the future
   c. A typical modern living room

3. Listen again. Answer the questions.
   1. How long has the EcoHouse been open?
   2. How many appliances are there in the living room?
   3. What does the museum use the EcoHouse for?
   4. Which appliances use the most energy?
   5. What did the experiment show?
   6. What does one student want to do at school?

### Vocabulary: Eco-construction verbs

4. Match the words with the definitions. Then listen and check your answers.

   1. _d_ install
   2. ___ build
   3. ___ design
   4. ___ reduce
   5. ___ discover
   6. ___ change
   7. ___ save
   8. ___ consume

   a. to make something by putting bricks or other materials together
   b. to stop someone or something from being killed or destroyed
   c. to find information, especially for the first time
   d. to put a piece of equipment somewhere and make it ready to use
   e. to use something such as a product, energy, or fuel
   f. to make something less
   g. to make or become different
   h. to draw or plan something, like clothes or buildings

5. **YOUR TURN** Work with a partner. Ask and answer the questions.
   1. What is one thing you could do to reduce trash at school and in your home?
   2. What do you think is going to be important when architects design new buildings in the future?
   3. Are architects the only ones who can discover new building techniques? Who else can participate in the process?

## Grammar: Simple past passive

**6. Complete the chart.**

Use the passive when it is not important who did the action, or when you don't know who did it.
To form the simple past passive, use was/were + past participle.

| Active | Passive |
|---|---|
| **Affirmative** | |
| We **built** the EcoHouse in 1985. | The EcoHouse **was built** in 1985. |
| We **updated** the appliances two months ago. | The appliances _____ **updated** two months ago. |
| **Negative** | |
| We **didn't install** a recycling bin until last year. | A recycling bin **wasn't** _____ until last year. |
| They **didn't install** solar panels 60 years ago. | Solar panels _____ **installed** 60 years ago. |
| Use by with the passive to show who did the action. | |
| The EcoHouse **was designed by** the museum. | |
| The most energy **was consumed by** the heater. | |
| **Questions and answers with the passive** | |
| When **was** the EcoHouse **built**? | It **was built** in 1985. |
| _____ the EcoHouse **built** in 1985? | Yes, it **was**. |
| **Were** the old apartments **destroyed** this year? | No, they **weren't**. |

> Check your answers: Grammar reference, p. 112

**7. Complete the paragraph with the simple past passive forms of the verbs.**

The building ¹ _was completed_ (complete) in 1985. It ² _____ (build) on a large piece of land outside the city. The air conditioners ³ _____ (install) 10 years ago. They ⁴ _____ (not put) in the bedrooms. The kitchen ⁵ _____ (redesign) two years ago.

**8. Rewrite the sentences using the simple past passive and *by*.**

1. The Spanish soccer team won the World Cup for the first time in 2010.
   _The World Cup was won by the Spanish soccer team for the first time in 2010._

2. The Chinese found dinosaur bones over 2,000 years ago in Sichuan.
   _____

3. Ray Tomlinson sent the first email in 1971.
   _____

## Speaking: Test your knowledge!

**9. Put the words in the correct order to make questions.**

1. by J. K. Rowling / written / *Romeo and Juliet* / Was / ?
   _____

2. the first *The Hunger Games* movie / was / When / released / ?
   _____

**10. YOUR TURN** Write four more questions of your own. Use the simple past passive. Then work with a partner. Ask and answer the questions in Exercise 9 and your own questions. Who knows the most answers?

> When was the first cell phone call made?

### Get it RIGHT!

Remember to include *was* or *were* in past passive sentences.
The building **was built** in 1985.
NOT: The building built in 1985.
People **were taught** to build homes quickly. NOT: People taught to build homes quickly.

Workbook, pp. 46–47

**REAL TALK** 7.2 WHAT KIND OF VOLUNTEER WORK CAN YOU DO IN YOUR SCHOOL OR TOWN?

# Be part of the SOLUTION.

**Conversation: What kind of volunteer work can you do in your school or town?**

1. **REAL TALK** Watch or listen to the teenagers. Which ideas for volunteer work would you like to do? Write 1–6 next to them; 1 is your favorite idea, and 6 is your least favorite idea.

   ___ join after-school clubs  ___ clean up trash
   ___ read to older people   ___ babysit
   ___ help older people with  ___ help in the school garden
   their animals

2. **YOUR TURN** Do you do volunteer work? What do you do, and why do you do it? If not, why not? Tell your partner.

3. Listen to James talking to Natalie. Complete the conversation.

**USEFUL LANGUAGE: Apologizing**
I didn't mean to | I'm really sorry. | It was my fault. | ✓ My apologies.

**Say it RIGHT!**
To make adjectives stronger, you can use words like *really*, *very*, and *extremely*. Put extra stress on these words. Listen and repeat the sentences.
I'm **really** sorry.
They were **very** noisy.
We're **extremely** excited!

**James:** Hey, Natalie. What happened to you yesterday?
**Natalie:** Yesterday? What do you mean?
**James:** Don't you remember? We agreed to go to the park and clean up trash? A whole bunch of us were there. You said you wanted to do it.
**Natalie:** Oh, no! ¹ _My apologies._ I forgot about that.
**James:** Natalie, I sent you a text to remind you!
**Natalie:** I know. ² _____ I didn't set my alarm clock.
**James:** You were supposed to bring trash bags. We were counting on you.
**Natalie:** ³ _____ What did you do?
**James:** I had to call my dad and ask him to bring us trash bags. He was pretty mad because he was busy with something else.
**Natalie:** ⁴ _____ forget. I feel really bad about that.
**James:** It's OK. We're doing it again next month. Can we count on you?
**Natalie:** Yes! I'll be there. I promise.

4. Practice the conversation with a partner.

5. **YOUR TURN** Work with a partner. Take turns apologizing to a friend and explaining what the problem was. Use the situations below.

**Situation A**
You forgot to help your friend read books to children at a library. Your friend had to do it alone.

**Situation B**
You didn't help your friend prepare a presentation for class about recycling. Your friend was up really late working on it.

# Volunteers Clean Valley Nature Reserve by Chris Davies

Last Sunday, about 100 people went to the Valley Nature Reserve to clean up the river. The event was organized by the Valley Conservation Society, which helps to protect the environment. Every year, local volunteers clean up trash that is thrown in the river. This year, I was one of them. We picked up hundreds of plastic bottles, plastic bags, and metal cans. That stuff was disgusting! The Society also removes non-native plants from the land near the river. These plants kill off native species and affect biodiversity. At the Valley Nature Reserve, we cut down kudzu, a pretty, but dangerous, plant. The cleanup was hard work, but it was fun. And the river looked great! Why not join us next time? We're already planning next year's event. It'll be in April. For more information, go to the Valley Nature Reserve website. ■

## Reading to write: Cleaning up a river

6. Look at the photo. What kind of trash did the volunteers find? Read the article and check.

> ● *Focus on* **CONTENT**
> **When you write a newspaper article, ask yourself these questions before you begin:**
> - What was the event?
> - When was it?
> - Where was it?
> - Who was involved?
> - What did they do?
> - What were the results?
> - What will happen next?

7. Underline the answers to the Focus on Context box questions in the article.

> ● *Focus on* **LANGUAGE**
> **Don't repeat the same word or words too much when you write. Use different words to refer to something you wrote about before.**
> *The event* = the Valley Nature Reserve cleanup
> *I was one of them* = one of the volunteers

8. Write what the words from the article refer to.
   1. *These plants* kill off native species: *non-native plants*
   2. *That stuff* was disgusting: _____
   3. . . . but *it* was fun: _____
   4. *It'll* be in April: _____
   5. a pretty but dangerous plant: _____

**Writing:** A newspaper article about an event

◻ **PLAN**
Plan your newspaper article about an event. Use the list in the Focus on Content box and make notes.

◻ **WRITE**
Write your article. Use your notes to help you. Write about 120 words.

◻ **CHECK**
Can you say "yes" to these questions?

- Is the information from the Focus on Content box in your article?
- Did you answer the questions from the Focus on Content box?

# UNDER THE AUSTRALIAN SUN

**A**ustralia is one of the sunniest countries on the planet, and sun is an important part of Australia's traditional outdoor lifestyle. Barbecues are held in sunny backyards 12 months a year. People spend days on end surfing at beautiful golden beaches. One in four homes has a swimming pool in the yard. You don't believe me? Look out the airplane window when you land at Sydney Airport. But there's more to sun than fun!

Australia gets more than 3,500 hours of sunlight a year – that's 10 hours a day – and solar energy is big business. Australia has invested enormously in solar energy. Solar panels provide energy to houses, schools, businesses, and factories all over the country. They have reduced the country's energy bills and had a very positive environmental impact.

However, there's a price to pay for so much sunshine. Rays from the sun can be very dangerous. The risk of skin cancer is high, so ads everywhere tell people to *Slip! Slop! Slap!* This very successful three-step approach was invented by experts to remind us what to use to protect our skin.

- ☀ First, *slip* on some special clothing. Clothes with special sun filters were invented by Australians and are really popular.
- ☀ Next, *slop* on some powerful sunscreen – even if you're only going out for 10 minutes. Use sunscreens with a sun protection factor (SPF) of at least 30+.
- ☀ Finally, *slap* on a big hat. Find a big hat that is designed so the sun doesn't hit your head or neck.

So remember, it's great to have fun in the sun, but wherever you are, and whatever you're doing – having a barbecue, chilling out at the pool, or surfing at the beach – don't forget to SLIP, SLOP, SLAP!

## Culture: Good sunshine, bad sunshine

1. Look at photos *a* and *b*. What can you see in each photo? What connects the two photos?
2. Read and listen to the article. Is the Australian attitude toward the sun mainly positive or mainly negative?
3. Read the article again. Answer the questions.
   1. How does the sun influence the Australian way of life?
   2. Why are solar panels successful in Australia?
   3. Why is the sun a problem in Australia?
   4. What are the three things you should slip on, slop on, and slap on?
4. **YOUR TURN** Work with a partner. Ask and answer the questions.
   1. Would you like to visit Australia? Why? / Why not?
   2. What's the sunniest place in your country?
   3. Is solar energy common in your country?
   4. How do you protect yourself from the sun?

### DID YOU KNOW...?
Eighty percent of Australians live within 50 kilometers of the coast.

**BE CURIOUS** Find out about a natural disaster in a town in Kansas, in the United States. How was the town different after it was rebuilt? (Workbook, p. 85)

7.3 BUILD IT BETTER

# UNIT 7 REVIEW

## Vocabulary

**1. Write the name of each material.**

 1
 2
 3
 4
 5
 6

1. G _L_ _A_ _S_ _S_
2. B __ __ __ __ __
3. W __ __ __ __
4. P __ __ __ __ __ __
5. P __ __ __ __ __
6. M __ __ __ __

## Grammar

**2. Rewrite the sentences. Use the simple present passive.**

1. They recycle these metal cans.
   _These metal cans are recycled._

2. They make these sweaters from plastic bottles.
   _____

3. They use corn to make heating oil.
   _____

4. They produce electricity from this water.
   _____

5. They build these houses from organic materials.
   _____

**3. Complete the questions and answers with the simple past passive forms of the verbs.**

| build | discover | ✓ make |
|---|---|---|
| destroy | grow | |

1. When _was_ the first talking movie _made_?
   It _was made_ in 1927.

2. When _____ tea first _____ in China?
   Tea _____ 4,000 years ago.

3. Where _____ gold _____ in the 1800s?
   Gold _____ in California in the 1800s.

4. When _____ Pompeii _____ by a volcanic eruption?
   Pompeii _____ by a volcanic eruption in 79 CE.

5. Where _____ the first public railways _____?
   The first public railways _____ in England in the 1800s.

## Useful language

**4. Complete the conversation.**

| really sorry | I didn't mean to | apologies | was my fault |
|---|---|---|---|

**Mom:** Kevin, don't throw out the soda cans and newspapers with the trash! We recycle those.

**Kevin:** Oh, yeah. I'm ¹_____. I totally forgot.

**Mom:** But we talked about this last month. Everyone in the house was going to help recycle. Remember?

**Kevin:** Yeah. My ²_____. I'll try to do better.

**Mom:** Thank you. Also, you have to clean the kitchen after you make snacks. Last night, it was a mess!

**Kevin:** Yeah, that ³_____. I made a snack and then went to bed. I was too tired to clean it up.

**Mom:** Kevin, come on.

**Kevin:** Sorry, Mom. ⁴_____ make you mad. It won't happen again.

---

**PROGRESS CHECK: Now I can . . .**

- ☐ identify materials.
- ☐ talk about how people recycle and reuse materials.
- ☐ talk about eco-construction.
- ☐ apologize.
- ☐ write a newspaper article.
- ☐ discuss solar energy and sun safety.

**CLIL PROJECT**

7.4 DRIVING INTO THE FUTURE, p. 119

# 8 Run for Cover!

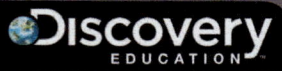

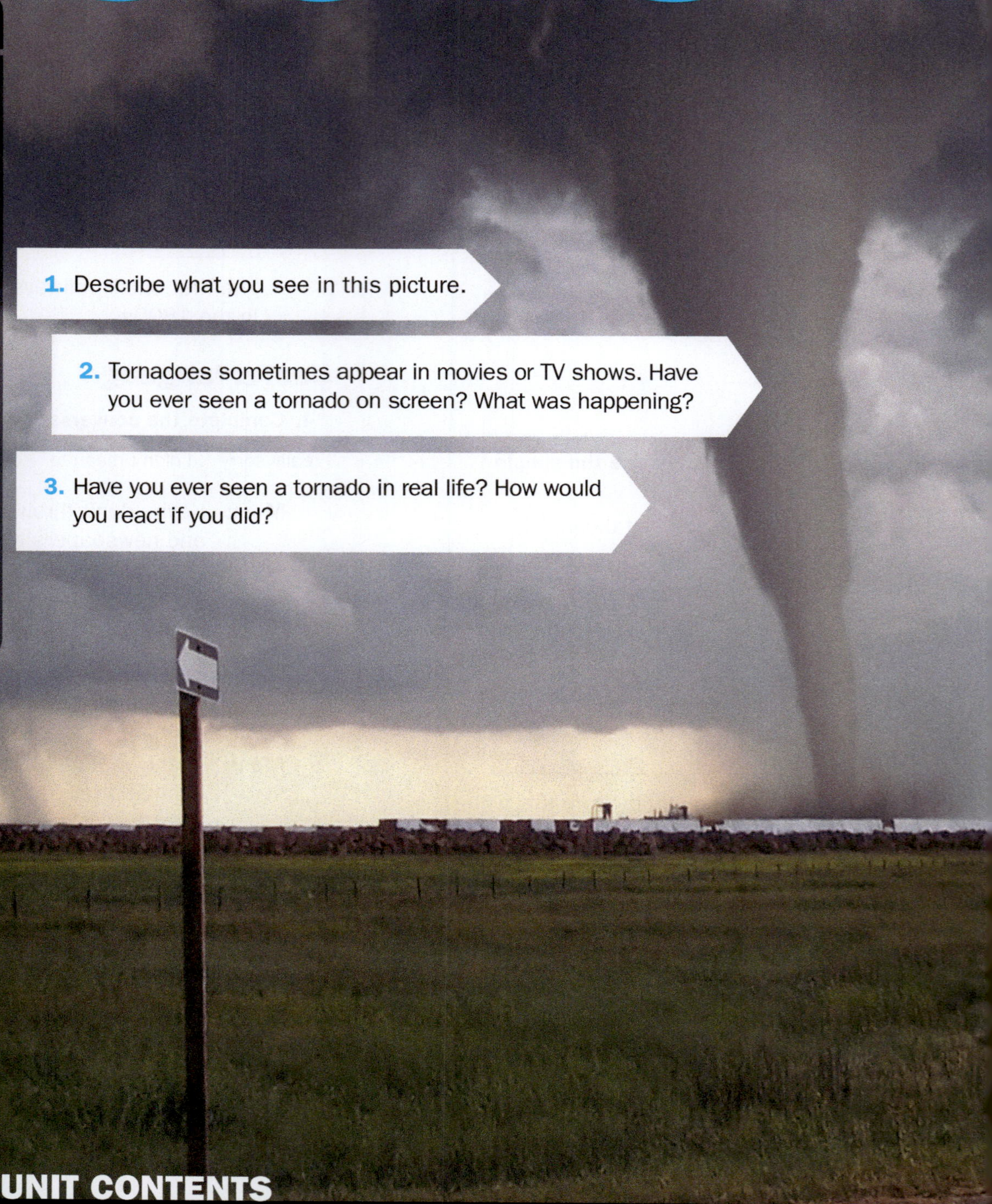

Discovery EDUCATION

BE CURIOUS

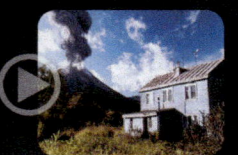

Land of Volcanoes

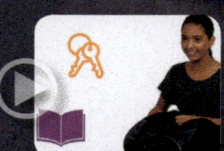

Do you often lose things?

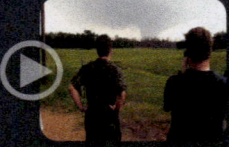

Storm Chasers

1. Describe what you see in this picture.
2. Tornadoes sometimes appear in movies or TV shows. Have you ever seen a tornado on screen? What was happening?
3. Have you ever seen a tornado in real life? How would you react if you did?

## UNIT CONTENTS

**Vocabulary** Natural disasters; survival essentials

**Grammar** Past perfect; past perfect *yes/no* questions; past perfect and simple past

**Listening** Survival story

## Vocabulary: Natural disasters

**1. Match the words with the correct pictures.**

1. _b_ tsunami
2. ___ volcanic eruption
3. ___ earthquake
4. ___ flood
5. ___ forest fire
6. ___ tornado
7. ___ hurricane
8. ___ landslide
9. ___ avalanche

**2. Listen, check, and repeat.**

**3. Match the news reports with disasters (a–i) from Exercise 1.**
1. "The wave is enormous. It's like a wall of water." ___
2. "The mountain is very dangerous. Rocks can fall at any time." ___
3. "The flames are now covering the hills, but people's homes are not in danger." ___
4. "The building is shaking. It's really frightening." ___
5. "I can see smoke and hot lava coming down the mountain." ___
6. "The funnel of wind pulled the roof off of a house, and it landed three kilometers away." ___

*Say it* **RIGHT!**

Pay attention to the pronunciation of these vowel sounds:
/æ/ dis**a**ster, l**a**ndslide, n**a**tural
/ɒ/ r**o**ck, imp**o**ssible, n**o**t
Find one more example of each sound in Exercise 3.
_____ _____

## Speaking: Terror or excitement?

**4. YOUR TURN Work with a partner. Ask and answer the questions.**
1. Which of the disasters from Exercise 1 are possible in your country?
2. What's the worst type of natural disaster, in your opinion? Why?
3. Do you know anyone who's experienced any of these disasters?
4. What's one more natural disaster not listed here?

> *Where we live, lots of these natural disasters are possible: earthquakes, floods, hurricanes, and landslides.*

Workbook, p. 50

**Reading** Krakatoa; Story Source; Chasing the Storms
**Conversation** Asking about and talking about personal problems
**Writing** A story about a personal experience

Unit 8 | 75

# The Loudest Sound in MODERN HISTORY

KRAKATOA

**W**hat's the loudest noise you can imagine? Double it and that might be close to the noise that the volcanoes on Krakatoa island made when they erupted in 1883. Scientific experts say that it was the loudest sound in modern history. People heard it in Australia, more than 3,000 kilometers away.

Krakatoa is a volcanic island between the islands of Java and Sumatra in Indonesia. When the volcanoes erupted, the explosions created a tsunami with waves more than 40 meters high. In fact, the tsunami caused more deaths than the volcanoes themselves. It killed 34,000 people and destroyed 165 towns and villages.

A huge cloud of dust traveled around the planet. As a result, the temperature of the world dropped one degree. The weather didn't return to normal until five years later, in 1888. People who saw the event said that the cloud had caused fantastic colors in the sky.

Terrible eruptions continued for weeks. Any survivors on other islands who hadn't escaped yet found out that they couldn't escape. They watched the explosions from a distance and organized festivals to celebrate the volcano. What had caused the eruptions? They didn't know. They also didn't know that the eruptions were so serious.

The Krakatoa volcano didn't erupt again until 1927. This eruption created a new island at the same location. There were more eruptions between 2009 and 2012, but they weren't dangerous.

Today, Indonesia has 130 active volcanoes – more than any other country in the world. So a new eruption is possible at any time!

## Reading: A magazine article

1. **Look at the title and the picture. What do you think the article is about?**

2. **Read and listen to the article. What was the loudest sound in history?**

3. **Read the article again. Are the sentences true (T) or false (F)?**
   1. The volcanoes on Krakatoa island erupted in 1883. ___
   2. More people died because of the tsunami than the volcanic eruptions. ___
   3. After the volcanic eruptions, the weather quickly returned to normal. ___
   4. People living on nearby islands knew exactly what caused the eruptions. ___
   5. Krakatoa had several dangerous eruptions between 2009 and 2012. ___
   6. No other countries have as many volcanoes as Indonesia. ___

4. **YOUR TURN  Work with a partner. Ask and answer the questions.**
   1. Why do you think there were climatic differences for five years after the volcano?
   2. Are there any areas with volcanoes in or near your country? Where are they? Are they still active?
   3. Have you heard about any recent volcanic eruptions or tsunamis? What do you remember about them?

### DID YOU KNOW...?
There are over 500 active volcanoes in the world. A large horseshoe-shaped area around the Pacific Ocean is called the "Ring of Fire." Over half the world's active volcanoes can be found there.

## Grammar: Past perfect

**5. Complete the chart.**

> Use the past perfect to refer to something that happened before a specific time in the past. To form the past perfect, use had + past participle.

| Affirmative | Negative |
|---|---|
| I was interested in Krakatoa because I **had read** a book about it. | I just read about Krakatoa. I **hadn't heard** about it before then. |
| The volcano _____ **been** fairly quiet for several years before the eruption. | I visited Indonesia last year. I _____ **been** there before, so it was new to me. |
| What _____ you **heard** about volcanoes before you visited one? Why _____**n't** you **researched** anything about Indonesia before you went there? | |
| **Contractions**   had = **'d**   had not = **hadn't** | |

> Check your answers: Grammar reference, p. 113

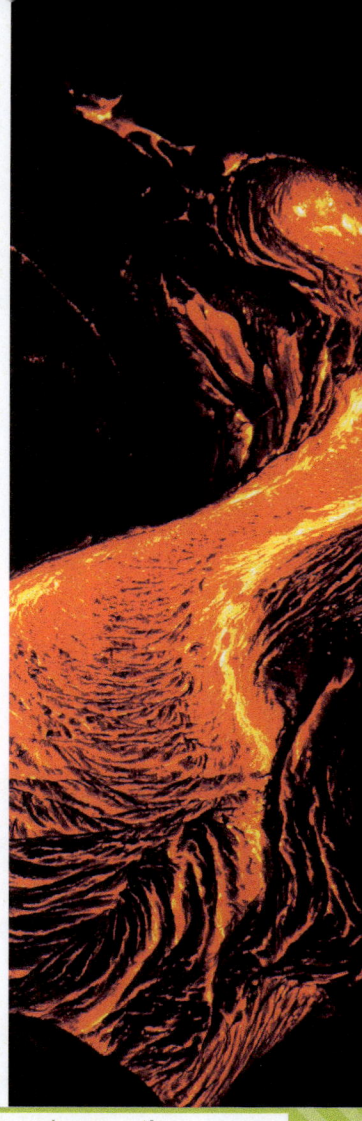

**6. Complete the sentences with the past perfect forms of the verbs.**

1. I _____ (read) about the volcanic eruption at Pompeii, but I didn't know much about Krakatoa.
2. Alan was surprised when he heard the thunder. When _____ the storm _____ (begin)?
3. We _____ (not have) an earthquake before 2004. Since then, we've had three!
4. There were two floods in our town last summer. Before that, I _____ (see) only one flood in 10 years.
5. Sadie went to Europe for the first time last summer. She _____ (not be) there before that.
6. I heard students laughing, and then I heard a loud noise. What _____ they _____ (do)?

**7. Put the words in the correct order to make questions.**

1. you / about Krakatoa / heard / today / before / had
   
   *Had you heard about Krakatoa before today?*

2. before the day of the show / had / bought the tickets / he
   
   _____

3. her teacher / Julie / had / met / before class started

| Past perfect yes/no questions | |
|---|---|
| **Had** you ever **seen** a tornado before you moved here? | Yes, I **had**. / No, I **hadn't**. |
| **Had** Amber **known** about the volcano on the next island? | Yes, she **had**. / No, she **hadn't**. |

   _____

4. had / before your parents came home / cleaned / you / your room

   _____

## Speaking: Before the disaster, . . .

**8. Imagine a volcano erupted 30 kilometers from your home. You and your family survived because you were prepared. Write three things you had done to prepare for the disaster.**

1. *Before the eruption, I had bought extra water.*
2. _____
3. _____

**BE CURIOUS** Find out about volcanoes in Russia. What is Sasha's job? (Workbook, p. 86)

**Discovery EDUCATION**
**8.1 LAND OF VOLCANOES**

**9. YOUR TURN Work in pairs. Talk about your preparations. Who was better prepared?**

> Before the eruption, I had bought extra water.

> That's good. I had forgotten that. But I had asked my mother to fill the gas tank of the car.

Workbook, p. 51

Unit 8 | 77

# Survival by ALL MEANS!

## Listening: Survival story

**1. Work with a partner. Ask and answer the questions.**
1. Do you enjoy exercising outdoors or walking in nature? Where have you done that and what was it like?
2. What kinds of things would you take with you if you were on a long hike or walking a long distance?

 **2. Listen to two friends discussing a news story about a hiker. Is it a happy or a sad story?**

 **3. Listen again. Answer the questions.** 
1. What's the climate in Queensland like?
   _____
2. What happened when the hiker was out running?
   _____
3. What was the weather like? 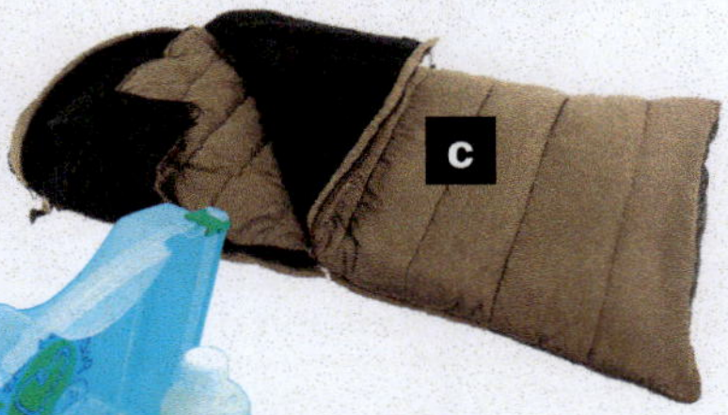
   _____
4. What had Sam brought with him?
   a bottle of _____, _____, _____, packs of _____ 
5. How did the contact lenses save him?
   _____
6. How did they find him in the end? 
   _____
7. How long was he lost?
   _____

## Vocabulary: Survival essentials

**4. Match the words and phrases with the correct pictures. Then listen and check your answers.**

1. ___ sunscreen
2. ___ water bottle
3. ___ sunglasses
4. ___ compass
5. ___ map
6. ___ sleeping bag
7. ___ penknife
8. ___ flashlight
9. ___ first-aid kit

**5. YOUR TURN Work with a partner. What's the most important survival equipment if you get lost in the following situations? Give reasons.**

a. In the mountains in the winter
b. In a forest at night
c. In the middle of a city

78 | Unit 8

## Grammar: Past perfect and simple past

**6. Read the sentences. Then circle the correct answer to complete the rules.**

> The young man's parents **called** the police after he **had been** gone for three days.
> The boy **had drunk** the liquid from all the contact lens cases when they **found** him.
> The boy **didn't tell** his story until he **had drunk** a lot of water.
>
> 1. We **can / can't** use the past perfect and the simple past in the same sentence.
> 2. We use the **simple past / past perfect** for the action that was completed first.

> Check your answers: Grammar reference, p. 113

**7. Circle the correct answers.**

1. Kent _____ about the weather until he _____ outside for a few minutes.
   a. didn't think / had been   b. had thought / had been

2. After Jen _____ her map for a long time, she _____ to turn left.
   a. studied / had decided   b. had studied / decided

3. The skier's family _____ worried only after the avalanche _____.
   a. had gotten / had happened   b. got / had happened

4. By the time my father _____, I _____ the party.
   a. had called / left   b. called / had left

**8. Complete the text with the simple past or past perfect forms of the verbs. Then listen and check your answers.**

I ¹___saw___ (see) an interesting movie last night. It was the true story of a guy named Aron Ralston. He was alone in a canyon in a national park. A large rock ²_____ (fall) on his right hand, and his hand was stuck between the rock and a wall. Unfortunately, before he ³_____ (leave) home, he ⁴_____ (not tell) his friends or family where he was going. They didn't know he was lost. He was in the canyon for five days. He ⁵_____ (drink) all his water already, and he ⁶_____ (eat) all his food, when he had an idea. He ⁷_____ (bring) along a small, cheap penknife, so he ⁸_____ (use) it to cut off his arm. It was terrible, but he did it. He was free. He started walking and found a family in the park. After they ⁹_____ (give) him some water, they ¹⁰_____ (call) emergency services. He survived! It was a very exciting story.

### Get it RIGHT!

Use the past perfect, not the present perfect, for referring to events completed before another past moment. *After I **had read** three books about forest fires, I decided to become a firefighter.* NOT: ~~After I **have read** three books about forest fires, I decided to become a firefighter.~~

## Speaking: I hadn't done my homework yet!

**9. Think about what you did yesterday. Write down one thing you had done, and one thing you hadn't done, by the time you did each thing in the box.**

| had breakfast | ate lunch | went to bed |
| got to school | had dinner | |

*By the time I had breakfast, I had taken a shower.*

**10. YOUR TURN Work with a partner. Ask and answer questions about the things you did.**

> Had you taken a shower by the time you had breakfast?

> Yes, I had. What about you?

> No, I hadn't. But I had made my bed.

Workbook, pp. 52–53

| REAL TALK | 8.2 DO YOU OFTEN LOSE THINGS? |

# Don't PANIC!

## Conversation: Do you often lose things?

1. **REAL TALK** Watch or listen to the teenagers. Check (✓) the things that are mentioned.

   ☐ cell phone ☐ sunglasses ☐ bike
   ☐ pencil ☐ remote control ☐ keys

2. **YOUR TURN** Do you often lose things? Tell your partner about things you have lost, what happened, and how you felt.

3. Listen to Adam and Daniela talking about a problem. Complete the conversation.

**USEFUL LANGUAGE: Asking about and talking about personal problems**

I don't know what to do!  ✓ What's the matter?  Don't panic!  Oh, no!  Let me think.

**Adam:** Hi, Daniela! [1] _What's the matter?_
**Daniela:** I can't find my backpack! It has all my books in it!
**Adam:** [2] _____ When did you last see it?
**Daniela:** I remember I put it in my locker before gym class.
**Adam:** Did you get it after gym?
**Daniela:** I don't remember. I went to the varsity basketball game right after that.
**Adam:** Did you have it at the game?
**Daniela:** I don't know. Maybe. I went to the mall with Emily. The game had finished, and we were hungry. And then we went to the park.
**Adam:** Did you leave it in the park?
**Daniela:** I'm not sure. I know Emily remembered her backpack. I asked her where she had bought it. But then I came home and when I realized I didn't have it, I went back. It wasn't there!
**Adam:** OK. [3] _____ Maybe you left it in the mall, in one of the stores.
**Daniela:** No, I don't think so. For one thing, no one has called me.
**Adam:** Had you written your name or phone number on your backpack?
**Daniela:** Yes. Now what? [4] _____
**Adam:** OK, hang on. [5] _____ OK, I have an idea. Let's go to the park and see if it's there. Then we'll go to the mall and ask for it at the Lost and Found. Then we'll go to school. Who knows? Maybe you left it in class.

4. Practice the conversation with a partner.

5. **YOUR TURN** Work with a partner. Describe a personal problem. Have your partner try to help you.

| Problem 1 | Problem 2 |
|---|---|
| You're at school. Your cell phone isn't in your bag. It's new, and it was expensive. It has all your friends' phone numbers in it and hundreds of pictures and songs. You had it this morning at home. | You're at a friend's house. You can't find your flash drive. It has all the work you did for a group presentation on it. You need it tomorrow. You had it earlier today at school. |

| Home | STORIES | Music | Movies |

## STORY SOURCE
Do you have a scary or difficult story to tell? Did you have a scary or difficult experience? Write and tell us what happened.

One afternoon last April, I was at home. I had turned the TV on and was about to watch my favorite show when suddenly, the electricity went off. Then my mom called to say that a tornado was in the area. Where I live, there are tornadoes every year, so, naturally, we had learned what to do at school.

We went down to the basement and hid in a closet. We could hear the storm, louder and louder, and then the walls started to shake. I had been a little scared the time before, but this time I was terrified. After about three minutes, when everything had become quiet again, we went to the kitchen to look outside. I saw that our house was OK, but unfortunately, the house next door was destroyed.

I called my mom immediately. My parents were safe, too. It was a horrible experience, but fortunately, we all survived.

## Reading to write: A blog about an experience

6. Look at the picture. What experience is the writer describing? What do you think your reaction to this experience would be?

   ◉ *Focus on* **CONTENT**
   **When you write about an experience, you can include this information:**
   - When it happened
   - Where you were
   - What happened
   - How you felt
   - The end of the story

7. Read the blog again. Underline the five pieces of information from the Focus on Content box.

   ◉ *Focus on* **LANGUAGE**
   **Adverbs**
   Use adverbs to link ideas together and make the story more dramatic and interesting.
   *. . . when **suddenly**, the electricity went off.*

8. Find four more examples of adverbs in the blog.

   *suddenly* _____  _____  _____  _____

9. Complete the sentences with the adverbs in Exercise 8.

   1. I had always lived in a place where there were hurricanes, so *naturally* I knew what to do when we heard the warning.
   2. We didn't wait for the authorities to tell us to leave when the floods started. We left _____.
   3. The earthquake was strong, but _____, there was no tsunami afterwards.
   4. _____ for our neighbors, the forest fire burned part of their house. It was ruined.
   5. Jeff was sleeping when _____, he heard a loud noise.

### Writing: A story about a personal experience

◯ **PLAN**
Plan your personal story for a website. Use the list in the Focus on Content box and make notes.

◯ **WRITE**
Write your story for the website. Use your notes and the blog to help you. Write about 120 words.

◯ **CHECK**
Can you say "yes" to these questions?
- Did you include the information from the Focus on Content box?
- Did you use adverbs like *suddenly* to make the writing more dramatic?

 Workbook, pp. 54–55

| Home | Stories | Music | Movies | Chat |

# CHASING THE STORMS

Tornadoes bring heavy rain and terrible winds – the strongest tornadoes travel at 400 kilometers per hour and are 80 kilometers wide. They are very destructive. Storm chasers are people who follow the tornadoes and try to get as close as possible. Today's interview is with Todd Robson, a storm chaser in Tornado Alley.

**What is Tornado Alley?**
It's the large area in the middle of the United States. It goes from Iowa in the north to Louisiana in the south. Most of the world's tornadoes happen in Tornado Alley. Every year, there are 1,000 or more tornadoes here!

**Why are there so many tornadoes in Tornado Alley?**
The summers are really hot, and there are lots of thunderstorms. Those are favorable conditions for tornadoes. Most tornadoes in Tornado Alley happen between March and August, but they can happen at any time of the year.

**What's it like living in Tornado Alley?**
New buildings in Tornado Alley have to have strong roofs and good foundations. A lot of people have special shelters underground – storm cellars – that protect them from tornadoes. And most neighborhoods have loud tornado sirens that warn them that a tornado is nearby.

**Why are you a storm chaser?**
Well, it's really exciting, but it isn't just a hobby. It's my job, too. Scientists need to understand storms better so that we can predict when they're coming and warn people.

**I've read about storm-chasing tours. Do they really exist?**
Yes! People can pay to go on storm-chasing trips. It's scary, and it can be a bit dangerous, but it's fun. Most of our tours are from April to June, and we drive all over Tornado Alley looking for storms. It's incredible!

## Culture: Tornado Alley

1. **Look at the photo. What kind of extreme weather do you see? What do you think the people in the car are doing?**

2. **Read and listen to the interview. Check your answers in Exercise 1.**

3. **Read the interview again. Complete the summary.**

   Todd Robson is a storm chaser in ¹_____. Tornadoes bring strong winds and ²_____. They can travel at ³_____. There are more than ⁴_____ tornadoes in Tornado Alley each year, where the summers are ⁵_____ and there are lots of thunderstorms. Many people have ⁶_____ that protect them from tornadoes. Some people chase storms because it's exciting, but scientists want to understand them better to ⁷_____ when they're coming. If you want to chase storms, the best time to do it is from ⁸_____ to June.

4. **YOUR TURN Work with a partner. Ask and answer the questions.**

   1. Why do you think people want to watch storms?
   2. Do you know anyone who's afraid of storms?
   3. Would you like to go on a storm-chasing tour? Why? / Why not?

### DID YOU KNOW...?
If you're near a tornado, the safest place is underground – in the basement of a house or in a special shelter.

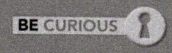

Find out about some scientists who study tornadoes. What is an F5 tornado? (Workbook, p. 87)

8.3 STORM CHASERS

# UNIT 8 REVIEW

## Vocabulary

**1. Match the words with the definitions.**

1. ___ earthquake
2. ___ avalanche
3. ___ hurricane
4. ___ eruption
5. ___ flood

a. powerful movements below the Earth's surface
b. an explosion inside a volcano
c. very strong winds that can cause a lot of damage
d. a large quantity of water that suddenly covers land and houses
e. a large quantity of ice or snow falling down a mountain

## Grammar

**2. Complete the paragraph with the past perfect forms of the verbs.**

| notice | read | see | ski | start | ✓ travel |

Last year, I was skiing in Utah with my family. We ¹ _had traveled_ to Utah before, but this was our first visit to this ski resort. My sister and I ² _____ avalanche warning signs in other areas, but there were no signs where we were that day. We ³ _____ down the hill, and a minute later, I heard a loud sound. I ⁴ _____ in a book that avalanches were loud, but this sounded like a train. A loud train! Suddenly, I saw a huge wall of snow coming down the hill after us. I shouted at my sister to ski fast and to follow me. We ⁵ _____ most of the way down the hill, as fast as we could go, when the avalanche reached us. We were covered in snow and couldn't find a way to escape. Luckily, some people ⁶ _____ us, and they had called a rescue crew.

**3. Complete the sentences and questions with the past perfect or simple present forms of the verbs.**

1. I _didn't see_ (not see) sharks until I _had left_ (leave) the ocean.
2. After we _____ (be) hiking for three hours, it _____ (start) raining.
3. The hikers _____ (not see) the landslide warning signs before they _____ (begin) walking down the hill.
4. The emergency workers _____ (not stop) looking for survivors until they _____ (make) sure everyone was safe.
5. She _____ (not drink) all the water in her bottle, so she _____ (share) some of it with her friend.
6. We _____ (feel) terrible when we saw all the houses the hurricane _____ (destroy).

## Useful language

**4. Complete the conversation.**

| don't | Let me | Oh | ✓ What's the | what to do |

**Maria:** Kate! Wake up! Look at that!
**Kate:** What? ¹ _What's the_ matter?
**Maria:** There's a spider in our tent. A big one. Look over there!
**Kate:** ² _____, no! Now what?
**Maria:** I don't know ³ _____! Do you?
**Kate:** Well, first of all, ⁴ _____ panic.
**Maria:** I'm trying not to. But look at it. It's huge!
**Kate:** I know. OK. Hang on. ⁵ _____ think.
**Maria:** Let's cover it with a towel and throw it outside.
**Kate:** Good idea. Get your towel.
**Maria:** My towel? Are you serious? Get your towel.
**Kate:** Maria, any towel is OK. Let's get going!

---

**PROGRESS CHECK: Now I can . . .**

☐ discuss natural disasters.
☐ ask and answer questions about past experiences.
☐ discuss past events.
☐ ask about and discuss personal problems.
☐ write about a difficult past experience.
☐ discuss tornadoes and people who chase tornadoes.

# 9 He SAID, She SAID

### Discovery EDUCATION

**BE CURIOUS**

Social Networks

What do you think about celebrity gossip?

The Language of the Future?

Pictures with Meaning

**1.** Describe what you see in this picture.

**2.** What kinds of things do you and your friends like to talk about?

**3.** When you're not together, how do you communicate with your friends?

## UNIT CONTENTS

**Vocabulary** Reporting verbs; Communication methods
**Grammar** Quoted speech vs. reported speech; reported questions
**Listening** Short conversations

## Vocabulary: Reporting verbs

**1. Match the words with the definitions.**

1. _e_ say — a. to speak very quietly (7 letters)
2. ___ explain — b. to express an idea for someone to consider (7 letters)
3. ___ remind — c. to say something very loudly (5 letters)
4. ___ whisper — d. to make someone remember something (6 letters)
5. ___ tell — e. to tell someone about a fact, thought, or opinion (3 letters)
6. ___ shout — f. to say you're unhappy or don't like something (8 letters)
7. ___ announce — g. to say you will certainly do something (7 letters)
8. ___ promise — h. to make something easy to understand (7 letters)
9. ___ suggest — i. to share news, stories, or information with someone (4 letters)
10. ___ complain — j. to say something officially (8 letters)

**2. Listen, check, and repeat.**

**3. Complete the sentences with words from Exercise 1.**

1. I usually forget to clean my room on Saturdays. My mother has to _remind_ me.
2. My brother's action figure was broken when he bought it. My father went to the store to _____, and he got his money back.
3. After my baby sister finally fell asleep, my mother asked us to _____ so we wouldn't wake her up.
4. I love it when my grandmother comes over. She likes to _____ me stories from when she was little.
5. Mr. Black is a great teacher. He can _____ really hard concepts so that we can understand them.
6. Jessica usually stays out too late, but this time she _____ her parents she would be home on time.

## Speaking: Tell about a time when you . . .

**4. YOUR TURN Work with a partner. Ask and answer the questions.**

1. When was the last time you shouted? Where were you, and why did you shout?
2. Do you know someone who complains a lot? Who? Do you usually agree with this person?
3. When was the last time you promised to do something? Did you do it? Why? / Why not?

> Once, when I was younger, I promised to make dinner with my little sister. We made dinner, but it was terrible!

### Say it RIGHT!

When a word ends in the final consonants *d*, *l*, *m*, and *n*, put your tongue in the position to say that letter, but don't say it. Native speakers put more emphasis on the vowel. Practice these sentences:
*I don't understan**d**. Can you please explai**n**?*
*There's nothing to te**ll**. He didn't come ho**m**e.*

Workbook, p. 58

**Reading** Communication Changes; Are Cell Phones Good for Teenagers?; The World Speaks One Language
**Conversation** Comparing different accounts of a story
**Writing** An essay about social networking sites

# The Reality of COMMUNICATION TODAY

## COMMUNICATION CHANGES
### by Amanda Mitchell

Teenagers love their cell phones and social networking sites, but there's conflict at home because of it. I talked to kids, parents, and experts to find out what's going on.

**1.** ___ "My cell phone is a great way for me to communicate with my friends," student Sarah Davis says. Sarah explained that she wanted to hang out with her friends after school – at the mall or in the park – but these days it wasn't easy. She said her mother, Becky, worried about her going out alone. "So, we go to social networking sites and hang out together that way." Becky isn't happy about it. "That's all she does," she complains.

**2.** ___ In the past 30 years, parents have become more concerned about security issues. Becky explained that kids in her generation hung out together every day. They rode their bikes to the mall, to each other's houses, or to the park. "But I just don't think that's safe anymore," she says.

**3.** ___ Psychologist Dr. Richard Turner said that conflict about cell phone use is becoming a common problem in families. "These kids grew up with cell phones. At the same time, parents are uncomfortable with the constant cell phone use. Obviously, families need to find a balance between safety concerns and a teenager's need to be with friends."

**4.** ___ Students are busier than they used to be. This is another reason why they spend time on social networking sites. "Universities like students who are active and engaged," student Mike Owens explains. That means that Mike does sports or other activities every day after school. "There's just no time to hang out with my friends. We use social networking sites instead," Mike laughs. He said that his parents sometimes get upset about this. "But what can I do? It's the reality!"

## Reading: A magazine article

1. **Read the possible paragraph headings for an article. What do you think the article is about?**

   a. Conflict in families
   b. Then and now
   c. No free time
   d. A great way to communicate

2. **Read and listen to the article. Match the headings (a–d) in Exercise 1 with the paragraphs.**

3. **Read the possible paragraph headings for an article again. Answer the questions.**

   1. Why isn't it easy for Sarah to hang out with her friends at the mall?
   2. Why does Becky complain about Sarah's cell phone use?
   3. Where did Becky and her friends hang out 30 years ago?
   4. What does Dr. Turner say is becoming a source of conflict in many families?
   5. What kind of students do universities look for?
   6. What does Mike do after school?

4. **YOUR TURN** Work with a partner. Ask and answer the questions.

   1. Where's your favorite place to hang out with your friends?
   2. What social networking sites do you use most? Why?
   3. What do you imagine social networking sites will be like in 10 years?

### DID YOU KNOW...?
The first handheld cell phones were used as car phones. They cost $4,000 to $9,000 in today's money and were so big and heavy that people called them "The Brick."

## Grammar: Quoted speech vs. reported speech

**5. Complete the chart with the words in the box.**

| can | Future with *will* | Present perfect | Simple past | ✓ Simple present |

*Use reported speech to tell others what another person said.*

| | | Quoted speech | Reported speech |
|---|---|---|---|
| 1. | Simple present | "It **isn't** right," she said. | She said that it **wasn't** right. |
| 2. | _____ | "We **spent** the whole day together," she told me. | She told me that they **had spent** the whole day together. |
| 3. | _____ | "We**'ve had** a cell phone for 12 years," he said. | He said that they **had had** a cell phone for 12 years. |
| 4. | _____ | "I**'ll text** you when I get to the party," he promised. | He promised that he **would text** me when he got to the party. |
| 5. | _____ | "I **can send** you an email," she whispered to her friend. | She whispered that she **could send** her friend an email. |

> Check your answers: Grammar reference, p. 114

**6. Look at the chart in Exercise 5. What does the verb in quoted speech change to in reported speech? Complete the table.**

| | Quoted speech | Reported speech |
|---|---|---|
| 1. | Simple present | Simple past |
| 2. | can | _____ |
| 3. | Present perfect | _____ |
| 4. | Simple past | _____ |
| 5. | will | _____ |

### NOTICE IT
In quoted speech, put the comma inside the quotation marks when the quote is first, and outside the quotation marks when the quote comes second.

"I'm using my computer right **now**," she said.
She **said,** "I'm using my computer right now."

**7. Write these sentences in reported speech form.**

1. "Social networking sites are a great way to talk to my friends," said Daniel.
   *Daniel said that social networking sites were a great way to talk to his friends.*

2. "I learned how to create video games," explained Sophie.
   _____

3. Mike announced, "Students can use their cell phones."
   _____

4. "I'll volunteer next Saturday," promised Sarah.
   _____

5. Travis said, "I've never been to Europe."
   _____

## Speaking: Face-to-face

**8. YOUR TURN** Work with a partner. Ask and answer the questions. Make notes of the answers your partner gives.

How often do you see your friends? What do you do together? Will you hang out this weekend?

**9.** Use your notes from Exercise 8 to write your partner's answers to the questions in reported speech. Then tell another pair of students about your partner.

> Jack said that he saw his friends on weekends and that they usually went to the mall. He said that they would go to the movies this weekend.

**BE CURIOUS** — Find out about social networks. What are the three social networking sites that the video talks about? (Workbook, p. 88)

**Discovery EDUCATION**
9.1 SOCIAL NETWORKS

Workbook, pp. 58–59

# Stop chatting and pay ATTENTION!

## Listening: Short conversations

1. **Work with a partner. Look at the four pictures. Ask and answer the questions.**
   1. Where are the people?
   2. What is the relationship between the people in each picture?
   3. What do you think they're talking about?

2. **Listen to four short conversations. Match the pictures in Exercise 1 to the conversations.**

   1. ____  2. ____  3. ____  4. ____

3. **Listen again. Answer the questions.**
   1. Nicole doesn't want to study. What does she want to do? Why does her mother think it's important to study hard?
   2. What is Joe texting Steve about? What does Joe think about his soccer skills?
   3. Why did Rachel have to go home? What did Rachel tell Mr. Peterson about the rules?
   4. Where are Paul and Addison going? What did Greg say would happen if they got to the concert early?

## Vocabulary: Communication methods

4. **Complete the sentences with the correct words. Then listen and check your answers.**

   | | | |
   |---|---|---|
   | blog post | forum | social network post |
   | chatting | ✓microblog post | text message |
   | email | phone call | video chat |

   1. My brother doesn't like to express himself in really short sentences, so he won't write a *microblog post*. He writes a long _____ every week, though, about whatever he's interested in.
   2. I can hear you pretty well, but I'm having trouble seeing you. I don't think the _____ is working. Let me send you an _____ instead.
   3. There was an article about the dress code on the school's online _____ today. I was _____ with Lisa about it in class, and Mr. Brown asked us to be quiet.
   4. It's been so long since I made a _____. I don't like to talk that much. I'd rather send a _____ from my phone.
   5. I like to write a _____ a few times a day to say how I'm feeling or to share funny videos with my friends.

5. **YOUR TURN** Work with a partner. What forms of communication do you like best? Why?

## Grammar: Reported questions

**6. Complete the chart.**

*In reported questions, the verbs usually change tenses as in reported speech.*
*The word order in reported questions is the same as in an affirmative sentence.*

| Direct speech questions | Reported questions |
|---|---|
| "Why **do** you **have** makeup on?" | He asked her why she ___had___ makeup on. |
| "Which blog post **did** you **read**?" | She asked me which blog post I _____. |
| "How **have** you **been**?" | He asked me how I _____. |
| "When **will** you **chat** with me?" | She asked me when I _____ with her. |
| "Who **can help** them send a text message?" | He asked who _____ them send a text message. |

*Use **if** in Yes/No reported questions.*

| | |
|---|---|
| "Are you on your way?" | He asked **if** we were on our way. |
| "Did you see what happened?" | She asked _____ I had seen what happened. |

> Check your answers: Grammar reference, p. 114

**7. Circle the correct answer.**

1. "Where is your cell phone?" She asked **if / where** my cell phone was.
2. "Will you write that blog post today?" My teacher asked **if / when** I would write that blog post today.
3. "Can you do a video chat with a cell phone?" My grandmother asked **can / if** I could do a video chat with a cell phone.
4. "What did you do last night during the game?" Leah asked **if / what** I had done last night during the game.

**8. Write the sentences as reported questions.**

1. Devon asked me, "How are you doing?"
   *Devon asked me how I was doing.*

2. Nicolas asked John, "Where have you been?"
   _____

3. My parents asked me, "Do you want to eat breakfast?"
   _____

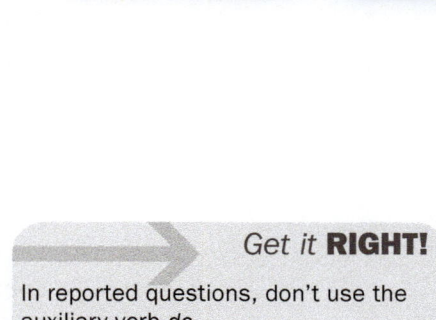

4. I asked my friends, "When can we hang out?"
   _____

### Get it RIGHT!
In reported questions, don't use the auxiliary verb *do*.
He asked me how **I created** my website.
NOT: ~~He asked me how **did I create** my website.~~

## Speaking: How often do you turn off your cell phone?

**9. Write five questions to ask your friends. Write about these things:**

| text | turn off your cell phone | video chat | write blog posts | write microblog posts |

**10. YOUR TURN** Work with a partner. Ask and answer your questions from Exercise 9.

> Have you ever written a blog post?
>> Yes, I have.

**11. Tell another pair of students about the questions your partner asked you.**

> Marco asked me if I had ever written a blog post.

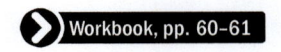

**REAL TALK** | 9.2 WHAT DO YOU THINK ABOUT CELEBRITY GOSSIP?

# That's not what I HEARD!

## Conversation: What do you think about celebrity gossip?

1. **REAL TALK** Watch or listen to the teenagers. Write the correct numbers.
   1. _____ of the teenagers said they didn't like celebrity gossip at all.
   2. _____ of the teenagers said that it depended on the situation or the topic.

2. **YOUR TURN** What do you think about celebrity gossip? Where do you hear the gossip you're interested in: social media, TV, online news, or another source?

3. Listen to Zoe and Cole talking about some celebrity news. Complete the conversation.

> **USEFUL LANGUAGE: Comparing different accounts of a story**
>
> That's not what I heard!  |  Well, Diana said that  |  That's definitely not what happened.  |  I asked Natalie what had happened, and she said that
>
> ✓ According to  |  How did you come up with that idea?

**Zoe:** ¹ _According to_ *Hollywood Tonight*, the police arrested Ashley Hill last night.

**Cole:** I heard that, too.

**Zoe:** It says that Ashley cut Jonah Clark's hair off while he was asleep, and then stole his car.

**Cole:** ² _____

**Zoe:** What? How do you know?

**Cole:** ³ _____ Ashley had borrowed her boyfriend's car. She didn't steal it. The problem is, she doesn't have a driver's license.

**Zoe:** She was probably with Shawn Evans when it happened.

**Cole:** Shawn Evans? ⁴ _____ She doesn't even know Shawn Evans.

**Zoe:** Yes, she does. They've been friends since they were on that TV show.

**Cole:** Oh yeah, that's right. Why do you think she was with Shawn last night?

**Zoe:** ⁵ _____ Shawn and Ashley are more than friends. They started dating about two weeks ago.

**Cole:** Where did Diana hear that? ⁶ _____ *Hollywood Tonight* just said that her boyfriend was Jonah Clark!

**Zoe:** This is pretty confusing. Let's see if Ashley posted anything online about it.

**Cole:** She can't post anything. She's in jail. Remember?

4. Practice the conversation with a partner.

5. **YOUR TURN** Work with a partner. Take turns comparing different accounts of the story.

> According to this site, Max Marker hit a photographer last night.

| Student A | Student B |
|---|---|
| You read online that your favorite singer got angry and tried to hit a photographer. | You hear from a friend that the photographer got angry and tried to hit your favorite singer. |

> No way. That's definitely not what happened. I heard that . . .

## ARE CELL PHONES GOOD FOR TEENAGERS?

by Avery Bradley

Twenty years ago, cell phones were mostly used by adults for work. Now, it's almost impossible to find a teenager without one. But are cell phones good for teenagers?

There are many good things about cell phones. First, they help teenagers communicate with friends and family anytime, anywhere. Sending text messages is quick and cheap. Cell phones also help organize your life – you have your calendar, photos, and social networking sites all in one place!

However, there are problems with cell phones, too. For one thing, if you forget to check your phone and miss text messages, your friends might think you're mad at them. In addition, you might not always get a signal, especially if you're not in a city. Finally, using your cell phone all the time can get really expensive.

Overall, I think cell phones are a great way for teenagers to communicate. We just need to be careful when we use them.

## Reading to write: An essay about cell phones

6. **Look at the title of the essay above. What do you think the essay is about? Read the essay to check.**

   ### ◉ Focus on CONTENT
   **When you write an essay, you can include this information:**
   - An introduction
   - A paragraph with arguments in favor
   - A paragraph with arguments against
   - A conclusion, including your opinion

7. **Read Avery's essay again. Answer the questions.**
   1. How does the writer get the reader's attention in the introduction?
   2. How many arguments in favor of cell phones are there?
   3. How many arguments against cell phones are there?
   4. What is Avery's opinion about cell phones for teenagers?

   ### ◉ Focus on LANGUAGE
   **Introducing a series of arguments**
   *First, In addition, For one thing, also, Finally*

8. **Find the phrases from the Focus on Language box in Avery's essay.**

9. **Complete the sentences with the correct words.**

   | also | finally | First |
   |---|---|---|
   | ✓ For one thing | In addition | |

   1. I recommend this cell phone. ¹ _For one thing_ , it's a smartphone. It's ² _____ on sale, and ³ _____, it's small and light.
   2. The new model has two improvements. ⁴ _____, it has a lot more memory. ⁵ _____, the battery will last longer.

### Writing: An essay about social networking sites

**◯ PLAN**
Plan an essay with the title "Are Social Networking Sites a Good Way for Teenagers to Communicate?" Use the list in the Focus on Content box and make notes.

**◯ WRITE**
Write your essay. Use your answers to Exercises 7 and 8 to help you. Write about 150 words.

**◯ CHECK**
Can you say "yes" to these questions?
- Have you included all the paragraphs mentioned in the Focus on Content box?
- Have you included words and phrases to introduce a series of arguments?

# THE WORLD SPEAKS ONE LANGUAGE

Almost everywhere you go in the world, you see English. It's on signs, advertisements, and on T-shirts. It's everywhere! Online, you see even more English. Why? Because it's a world language: a language known and spoken in lots of countries.

How many people speak and understand English? Statistics show that there are 375 million native speakers of English in the world. In some places, like India, Hong Kong, and Kenya, people speak lots of different languages, and English is one of them. Finally, linguists have said that there are more than a billion people who speak English as a foreign language, and that figure is increasing. In many countries, such as Denmark, Singapore, and Israel, more than 80 percent of the people speak English.

Do you like to travel? International tourists can't speak the language of every country they dream of visiting. Most countries, however, write signs, menus, and tourist pamphlets in at least two languages: the native language of that country and English. Tourists may not speak Arabic, for example, but when they visit Egypt, they can still eat great food, take tours, and have a wonderful time if they speak English.

Online, English is important, too. In 2013, researchers said that 55 percent of the most popular websites used English as their main language. If you set up a blog, for example, more people will find out about you and read your posts if you write in English. Over 95 percent of all scientific articles, either online or published in science magazines, are in English. And that number is growing.

And what about the future? Will English always be the world's number one language? For the moment, yes. But if the Chinese economy continues to grow, will Mandarin turn into the next number one world language? We'll have to wait and see.

## Culture: The number one language

1. **Look at the photo above. Where would you see this sign? Why do you think the sign is in English?**

2. **Read and listen to the article. Is English still the world's number one language?**

3. **Read the article again. Are the sentences true (*T*) or false (*F*)?**
   1. English is everywhere because it's a world language. ___
   2. About 375 million people speak English as a foreign language. ___
   3. Most countries try to help tourists by creating material in English. ___
   4. Over half of the most popular websites use English as the main language. ___
   5. The author is sure that Mandarin will be the world's next number one language. ___

4. **YOUR TURN** Work with a partner. Ask and answer the questions.
   1. How much English do you see or hear where you live? Where do you see it?
   2. Do you ever use English on the computer or on your phone? What do you use it for?

### DID YOU KNOW...?
Soon there will be more people in China who speak English as a foreign language than there are native English speakers in the whole world.

**BE CURIOUS** Find out about the Mandarin language. How many written characters are there in Mandarin, and how many do most people use? (Workbook, p. 89)

**Discovery EDUCATION**
9.3 THE LANGUAGE OF THE FUTURE?

# UNIT 9 REVIEW

## Vocabulary

**1. Complete the sentences with the correct words.**

| announce | ✓explain | shout |
| complain | remind | whisper |

1. I don't understand our homework. Can you ___explain___ it to me?
2. Ken and Emily often _____ about people who use cell phones all the time. They really don't like it.
3. The fans in the stadium usually _____ so loudly that the other team can't hear instructions from the coach.
4. Please don't talk loudly here! People are studying, and you need to _____.
5. When are the TV stations going to _____ the news about the election?
6. If I don't remember to call my mom, please _____ me.

## Grammar

**2. Rewrite the sentences below in reported speech.**

1. "I'm blogging about the movie."
   _She said she was blogging about the movie._
2. "I go online every day."
   He _____.
3. "I can video chat with you tonight."
   She _____.
4. "I have written 100 blog posts."
   He _____.
5. "I am thinking about Daniel."
   She _____.
6. "I will send Paul an email."
   He _____.

**3. Rewrite the questions below as reported questions.**

1. "Who are you talking to?"
   She _asked who I was talking to._
2. "What is Alicia thinking about?"
   He _____
3. "Do you have Will's phone number?"
   They _____
4. "When will he send them a text message?"
   She _____
5. "Have you posted the picture on your blog?"
   He _____
6. "Who can help her?"
   They _____

## Useful language

**4. Complete the conversation.**

| According to | That's definitely |
| Steve said that | That's not |

**Tyler:** Hey, Rob. I just heard about Ryan.
**Rob:** What did you hear?
**Tyler:** ¹_____ Ryan had been cheating on a test with his cell phone, and Ms. Harris caught him.
**Rob:** ²_____ not what happened.
**Tyler:** What do you mean?
**Rob:** ³_____ Jared, Ryan saw someone else cheating, and he told Ms. Harris about it.
**Tyler:** Hmm. ⁴_____ what I heard.
**Rob:** Ryan never cheats. And, I don't think he even has a cell phone. He lost his last week.
**Tyler:** Well, where is Ryan now? Let's just ask him and find out the truth!

---

**PROGRESS CHECK: Now I can . . .**

- ☐ talk about different ways of speaking.
- ☐ discuss social networking.
- ☐ talk about different communication methods.
- ☐ compare stories.
- ☐ write an essay about cell phones.
- ☐ discuss language use throughout the world.

**CLIL PROJECT**
9.4 PICTURES WITH MEANING, p. 120

# 10 Don't Give Up!

## Discovery EDUCATION
### BE CURIOUS

- Lifeguard and Athlete 
- Have you ever given a class presentation? 
- Circus Star

1. Describe what you see in this picture.

2. What do you think this runner did to prepare for the race?

3. Have you ever worked very hard toward a specific goal? What did you do?

## UNIT CONTENTS

**Vocabulary** Goals and achievements; emotions related to accomplishments
**Grammar** Reflexive pronouns; causative *have/get*
**Listening** Challenging situations

## Vocabulary: Goals and achievements

**1. Write the words next to the definitions.**

| achieve | commitment | face | performance | reward |
|---------|------------|------|-------------|--------|
| challenge | ✓ deal with | goal | progress | skill |

1. To take action to solve a problem: D E A L  W I T H
2. Something you want to do successfully in the future: _ _ _ _
3. How well someone does something: _ _ _ _ _ _ _ _ _ _ _
4. To succeed in doing something good: _ _ _ _ _ _ _
5. To give something in exchange for good behavior or good work: _ _ _ _ _ _
6. To deal with a difficult situation: _ _ _ _
7. An ability to do an activity well because you have practiced it: _ _ _ _ _
8. Development and improvement of skills or knowledge: _ _ _ _ _ _ _ _
9. Something that is difficult and tests your ability: _ _ _ _ _ _ _ _ _
10. A willingness to give your time and energy: _ _ _ _ _ _ _ _ _ _

**2. Listen, check, and repeat.**

**3. Circle the correct answers.**

1. You ran 5 kilometers last week and 10 kilometers this week. That's real **progress / goal**!
2. My father **dealt with / achieved** something no one in his family had done before: He went to college and became a doctor.
3. Your **commitment / performance** on this test was incredible. You got 100 percent right!
4. This class isn't easy. It will **challenge / achieve** you to work harder than you've ever worked before.
5. Bianca didn't study for her chemistry test, so she had to **reward / face** the consequences: a bad grade.
6. My **goal / skill** in life isn't to be rich or famous. I just want to be good at what I do.

> **Spell it RIGHT!**
> Notice that *ie* and *ei* can both represent the sound /iː/.
> ach*ie*ve, bel*ie*ve
> c*ei*ling, rec*ei*ve

## Speaking: Go for it!

**4. YOUR TURN Work with a partner. Ask and answer the questions.**

1. What is one academic or personal goal that you have for the next 12 months?
2. Do you have an unusual skill? What is it?
3. Have you ever been challenged to do a difficult or incredible thing? What?

> One of my academic goals for the next 12 months is to get better grades in science.

▶ Workbook, p. 64

**Reading** Make Your Dreams Come True; Achieving My Goal; Olympics for the Brain
**Conversation** Reassuring someone
**Writing** A personal action plan

# Dream BIG!

## Make Your DREAMS Come True

by Kyle Stewart, school counselor at West High School in Franklin, Pennsylvania

In my 22 years as a high school counselor, I've talked to thousands of teenagers. Many of them have goals, from traveling around the world to changing the world. While some teenagers achieve the goals they set for themselves, others don't. If you have a dream, here's how to make it happen:

First, decide on a clear goal. What exactly do you want to do? Make sure it's your dream and not someone else's. Your father wants you to be a doctor. Do you want to be a doctor, too? If you do, great. You will need your own commitment to do the hard work of reaching your long-term goals.

Then choose a date to reach your goal. For example, do you want to go to college a year early? Then you may want to take extra classes now. Set a deadline, and challenge yourself to meet that deadline.

I've found that most people benefit from writing about their goals. A written list reminds people to work on their goals and helps them see their progress! Start by writing down your goal, your deadline, and the steps you need to take to make your dream a reality.

Finally, put your plan into action. Start taking the steps you wrote on your list. You have to do this work yourself. No one can do it for you. Remember to review your written goals at least once a week. And then, dream your dreams and never give up!

## Reading: An online article

1. Look at the title of the article. Do you have a dream that you'd like to come true? What could you do about it?

2. Read and listen to the article. Number the steps below in the correct order (1–4).
   a. ___ Set a date to accomplish your goal.
   b. ___ Make your plan happen.
   c. ___ Decide for yourself what your goal is.
   d. ___ Get a pen and paper and start writing.

3. Read the article again. Are the sentences true (*T*) or false (*F*)?
   1. Kyle Stewart is a teenager with a dream. ___
   2. All of the students that Kyle talks to achieve their dreams. ___
   3. It's important to make sure that your goal is something you want for yourself. ___
   4. Students should decide a date by which they want to achieve their goal. ___
   5. Writing down the goal is not an important step. ___
   6. Nobody else can put your plan into action. You have to do it. ___

4. **YOUR TURN** Choose one of the goals below or a goal of your own. How could you achieve this goal? Discuss your steps with a partner.

| | | |
|---|---|---|
| be a scientist | improve your grades | make new friends |
| get fit and healthy | learn a musical instrument | save the environment |

> *I want to make some new friends, and I want to do it by the end of this year.*

> *Maybe you could join a new club!*

### DID YOU KNOW...?

The first jobs of many famous people were very different from their dreams. Singer Mick Jagger worked in a mental hospital, actress Jennifer Aniston was a telephone salesperson, and actor Tom Hanks sold popcorn and peanuts.

## Grammar: Reflexive pronouns

**5. Complete the chart.**

> *Use a reflexive pronoun when an object refers to the subject.*
> **I** like to challenge **myself** by measuring my progress every week.
> **You** need to set a deadline for _____.
> **He** wasn't pleased with **himself** when he heard criticism of his performance.
> **She** taught _____ the skills she needed to write essays.
> **We** decided to enjoy **ourselves** only after we had studied for the test.
> **Teenagers** can help _____ to any of the career planning books we have.
> Many people achieve the goals **they** set for **themselves**.

> Check your answers: Grammar reference, p. 115

**6. Complete the sentences.**

1. My sister rewarded __*herself*__ with a long walk after she had studied for three hours.
2. We set _____ a deadline for finishing the big project.
3. I didn't do well on the test. I blame _____ for not studying harder.
4. To succeed in life, you need to believe in _____.
5. Those kids need to face challenges by _____. They can't always ask their parents to help them.
6. Edward scared _____ when he thought he had lost his homework.

**7. Add a sentence with a reflexive pronoun and *by*.**

1. Nobody in the group had time to work on the presentation except Adrian and Stephanie.
   *They worked on it by themselves.*
2. He didn't have help writing his essays for school.
   _____
3. Nobody helped Cristina do the project.
   _____
4. None of my friends wanted to study with me yesterday.
   _____
5. My sister and I didn't do our exchange programs together.
   _____
6. My best friend couldn't go shopping yesterday.
   _____

> **Reflexive pronouns with *by***
>
> *You can use reflexive pronouns with by to say you did something "without help" or "alone."*
>
> I don't cook much, but I made this dinner **by myself**. Do you like it?
>
> Mike painted his house **by himself**. He didn't hire a professional painter.

## Speaking: Achieve it!

**8. YOUR TURN Work with a partner. Choose one of the goals below. Decide on five steps a person needs to take to achieve it.**

a. Win a gold medal in the Olympic Games
b. Discover a cure for cancer
c. Win an Oscar for best actor in a movie

> *To win a gold medal, you have to challenge yourself.*

> *Right, but you can't do it all by yourself. You need a coach!*

### Say it RIGHT!

10.03

A consonant cluster is a group of consonants with no vowels. Pay attention to the pronunciation of consonant clusters with /l/. Listen and repeat the words.
mys**elf**, hims**elf**, thems**elves**
ski**lls**, she**lls**, te**lls**

**BE CURIOUS** Find out about a lifeguard in Australia. What does Candice do to train for the life saving competition? (Workbook, p. 90)

**Discovery EDUCATION**
10.1 LIFEGUARD AND ATHLETE

Workbook, p. 65

Unit 10 | 97

# Are you up to the CHALLENGE?

## Listening: Challenging situations

1. Look at the topics below. How could they be "challenging situations"?
   a. A homemade birthday cake
   b. A video competition
   c. An important test
   d. A soccer championship

2. 🔊 10.04 Listen to four short conversations. Match the topics in Exercise 1 with the conversations.

   1. _____   2. _____   3. _____   4. _____

3. 🔊 10.04 Listen again. Answer the questions.
   1. What did Lauren and her team win? Why isn't Lauren jumping up and down?
   2. What was the name of the competition that David entered? What bad thing happened while David was making the video?
   3. Who is Jennifer making the birthday cake for? What kind of cake is Jennifer's friend going to have made?
   4. Why had Logan missed a lot of school? Where is Logan's dad going to take him?

## Vocabulary: Emotions related to accomplishments

4. 🔊 10.05 Complete the sentences with the correct words.

   | calm | ✓ disappointed | miserable | prepared | satisfied |
   |---|---|---|---|---|
   | confident | excited | nervous | proud | thrilled |

   1. I'm _disappointed_ that I can't be in the play. I really wanted to do it.
   2. After training every day for seven weeks, I know I'm _____ for the race.
   3. I was _____ of my son for doing his homework every day this week.
   4. Sabrina studied really hard for the test, so she was _____ that she would do well.
   5. My sister got an amazing scholarship to a school in Australia. She's _____!
   6. Don't worry so much about your presentation. Just stay _____.
   7. I could get a new bike, but I'm pretty _____ with my old one.
   8. I was so _____ about my new school that I couldn't sleep the night before the first day of classes.
   9. Vince can't go to summer camp this year, and he feels _____ about it.
   10. When I'm _____ about something, I wake up really early and have lots of energy.

5. **YOUR TURN** Choose five words from Exercise 4. For each word, tell a partner about a time you felt that emotion.

## Grammar: Causative have/get

**5. Complete the chart.**

| |
|---|
| Use causative have/get in situations where someone else does something for you. You don't do it. You can use get or have. They have similar meanings. |
| Lauren is **getting** her knee **examined** now. (She isn't examining her own knee. A doctor is.) |
| Jennifer **had** a cake _____ for her friend. (She didn't make it. A professional did.) |
| David needs to **get** his camera _____. (He can't fix it. A professional can.) |
| Logan will **have** his eyes _____. (He won't check them. A professional will.) |
| The past participle of get is gotten. |
| Has Sophia **gotten** Jason's cake made yet? No, she hasn't. |

> Check your answers: Grammar reference, p. 115

**6. Complete the sentences with causative have/get and the words in parentheses.**

1. Derek gets bad headaches every night when he does his homework. He needs to ___get his eyes checked___ (check his eyes).

2. Veronica needed a photo of herself for her passport. She went to a photographer to _____ (take her photo).

3. To look good for the school dance, I'm going to _____ (cut my hair) this afternoon.

4. I'm going to _____ (paint my bedroom) bright pink so that I feel more motivated to study.

5. Your sister is really smart! Has she _____ (test) to see if she has an extra-high IQ?

6. Jim wasn't confident about the game because his shoulder hurt a lot. He should have _____ (examine his shoulder) before the game.

**7. Read the situations and write sentences with causative have/get.**

1. Mitch's only dress shirt is dirty. A dry cleaning company washed it.
   _He got his shirt cleaned._

2. My computer is broken, and I really need it. A repair person is going to fix it tomorrow.
   _____

3. The cheerleader hurt her knee. A doctor bandaged it.
   _____

4. The students stayed up late getting their English project ready. A pizza place delivered a pizza to them.
   _____

### Get it RIGHT!

When you get/have something done, you don't do it yourself.
I'm going to cut my hair. = I'm going to cut my own hair.
I'm going to get/have my hair cut. = Another person is going to cut my hair.

## Speaking: Let's have a party!

**8. YOUR TURN** Work with a partner. Choose one of the events below. Decide on six steps to make the event happen. You must do three by yourselves, and get other people to do three.

a. You're going to have a birthday party, and you will invite 200 people.
b. You're going to organize a concert where a local band will play for your community.
c. You're in charge of a school trip. Three classes are going together to visit an important monument or nature site outside your city.

> For this birthday party, we need to get 200 invitations printed.

Workbook, pp. 66–67

**REAL TALK** 10.2 HAVE YOU EVER GIVEN A CLASS PRESENTATION?

# You'll do GREAT!

## Conversation: Have you ever given a class presentation?

1. **REAL TALK** Watch or listen to the teenagers. Write the numbers 1–6 in the order that you hear about these things.

   a. ___ I'm worried about doing one.
   b. ___ We talked about summer camp.
   c. _1_ I talked about Indonesia last week.
   d. ___ We do one every Friday.
   e. ___ I don't know how to surf.
   f. ___ I talked about my family and friends.

2. **YOUR TURN** Have you ever given a class presentation? What was the best part? What was the worst?

3. Listen to Julia talking to her sister Ella about a presentation. Complete the conversation.

   **USEFUL LANGUAGE: Reassuring someone**
   - I think I can help you.
   - ✓ You've faced bigger challenges than this!
   - Try not to worry about it.
   - I'm sure you'll do fine.

   **Julia:** What's the matter, Ella? You look miserable.
   **Ella:** I'm not miserable, just nervous. I have to give a presentation in English class next week, and I'm scared.
   **Julia:** Come on. A presentation? ¹ _You've faced bigger challenges than this!_
   **Ella:** Yeah, but not in English. And never in front of people!
   **Julia:** ² _____ Your English is good.
   **Ella:** Yes, but I'm really shy. And some people in my class speak really great English. I'm worried they'll laugh at me.
   **Julia:** You'll do great.
   **Ella:** No, I won't! When I speak in class, I mix up the words and talk too fast.
   **Julia:** Listen, ³ _____ Have you written the presentation yet?
   **Ella:** Well, most of it. It's almost done.
   **Julia:** Great, then. You can practice it on me and my friends. The more you practice, the better you'll do.
   **Ella:** OK! That sounds like a good idea. I'll feel more confident then.
   **Julia:** Exactly. ⁴ _____ You'll be fine.

4. Practice the conversation with a partner.

5. **YOUR TURN** Work with a partner. Take turns explaining one of the problems and reassuring your partner.
   - You have to sing a song in a talent show.
   - You're playing in the final of a tennis tournament.

# Achieving MY GOAL

Posted by Jacob, October 15

In two years, when I'm 17, I am determined to be an exchange student in a Spanish-speaking country. In order to achieve this, I will begin taking Spanish classes next semester at school. I don't speak any Spanish, so I'll have to study hard every day. In addition, I'll do research on different study abroad programs. When I find the best one, and learn about the price and the way it works, I'll talk to my parents. I'll need help from them, and I hope they agree to help! I'll ask them if they can pay for part of the program. I also plan to get a job in the summer – this summer and the next. I'll work as much as I can and keep studying Spanish. Then I'll apply for the exchange program, filling out all the forms and getting all the documents needed. When I'm accepted, I'll apply for my passport, and a visa if necessary. Finally, the program will tell me what country I'm going to – Spain, Mexico, Argentina, or Peru. I'll study about the history and culture of that country. That way, I'll be really prepared.

## Reading to write: Jacob's blog post

6. Look at the picture. What do you think Jacob's goal is? Read his action plan and check.

> ● *Focus on* **CONTENT**
> When you write about a goal, begin by describing your goal clearly. Then describe each step you need to take to achieve your goal. For some of the steps, you may need help from other people. Tell your readers who those people are and how they'll help you.

7. Read Jacob's blog post again. Number the steps (1–7) in the order he will take them.

   a. ___ talk to his parents
   b. ___ get a job
   c. ___ start Spanish classes
   d. ___ learn about the country
   e. ___ apply for the program
   f. ___ research programs
   g. ___ apply for a passport and visa

> ● *Focus on* **LANGUAGE**
> When you write about a personal action plan, you can include some of these phrases:
> *I am determined to . . .*
> *In order to achieve this, I will . . .*
> *In addition, I will . . .*
> *I will need help from . . .*

8. Find the phrases in the Focus on Language box in Jacob's blog post and underline the entire sentence.

## Writing: A personal action plan

◻ **PLAN**
Choose a goal you'd like to achieve. Write what the goal is and at least five steps toward achieving the goal.

◻ **WRITE**
Write your personal action plan. Use your notes from above to help you. You can also use Jason's blog post as a model.

◻ **CHECK**
Check your writing. Can you say "yes" to these questions?

- Is your goal described clearly?
- Did you write at least five steps toward your goal?

# Olympics for the Brain

Do you want to win medals and earn scholarships? These things are not just for great athletes, but for hard-working students, too. How? Form a team and join Academic Decathlon®!

## What is Academic Decathlon®?
It's an academic competition for students from all over the United States, and sometimes all over the world. Every year, teams of students study one topic – past themes have included Russia, the Great Depression, and energy alternatives. Then they compete in local, state, and national championships.

## Who is on each team?
Teams include nine students, and each team must have three different types of students on it. Three members must be excellent students. Three members must be students who do well, but who aren't the school's top students. And three team members must be students who don't get great grades.

## What happens in the competition?
Competitions aren't about being good at one subject area only. Every team member needs to be prepared to do five things. First, they need to deliver a speech related to the topic, and then answer questions. Then students need to answer questions about themselves in an interview. After that, they need to write an essay about the topic. They also need to take seven different tests in subject areas related to the topic. And finally, teams participate in a Super Quiz. Teams listen to questions and have seven seconds to answer them. It's the only part of the competition open to the public, and it's noisy, fun, and exciting.

## Why do students love Academic Decathlon®?
Lots of reasons! Like athletes, these students enjoy working as a team. If you join a team, you'll meet other students from all over the country, and work very hard to get there. Most of all, you'll have fun!

## Culture: United States Academic Decathlon®

1. **Answer the questions.**
   1. Have you ever won a medal? What was it for?
   2. Would you be interested in participating in an academic competition?

2. **Read and listen to the article. What kinds of students can participate in Academic Decathlon®?**

3. **Read the article again. Answer the questions.**
   1. Where do the students who compete come from?
   2. How many people are on a team?
   3. Do team members need to learn about one subject area or all subject areas?
   4. What do students have to answer questions about in the interview?
   5. Which part of the competition can the public watch?

4. **YOUR TURN** Work with a partner. Ask and answer the questions.
   1. What kind of academic competitions can you compete in where you live?
   2. Would you enjoy participating in Academic Decathlon®? What part of it sounds most interesting to you?

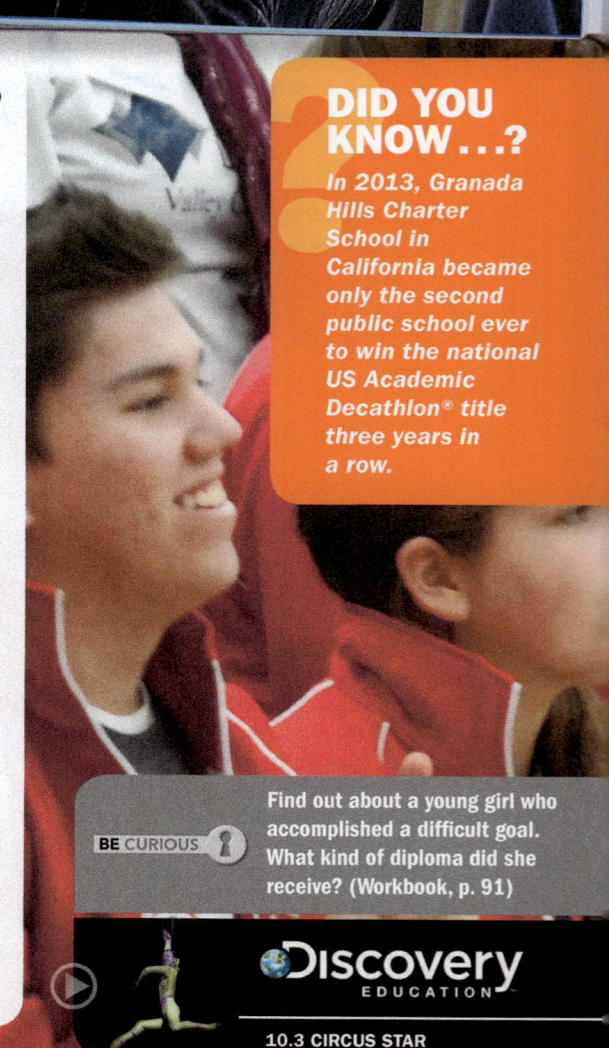

### DID YOU KNOW...?
In 2013, Granada Hills Charter School in California became only the second public school ever to win the national US Academic Decathlon® title three years in a row.

**BE CURIOUS** Find out about a young girl who accomplished a difficult goal. What kind of diploma did she receive? (Workbook, p. 91)

Discovery EDUCATION
10.3 CIRCUS STAR

# UNIT 10 REVIEW

## Vocabulary

**1. Complete the sentences.**

| challenge | goal | rewarded |
|---|---|---|
| face | progress | ✓ skills |

1. Academic Decathlon® helps students develop their public speaking ___skills___.
2. When you want to accomplish an important _____, it's a good idea to write it down and look at it often.
3. Caleb doesn't like to do only easy things. He likes to _____ himself.
4. After several students in my class won an academic competition, the school _____ the whole class with a party.
5. You won't achieve your goal right away, but you can make a little _____ toward it every day.
6. Instead of ignoring or running away from your problems, it's always better to _____ them directly.

## Grammar

**2. Complete the sentences with reflexive pronouns.**

1. After doing homework for seven hours on Saturday, Greta rewarded ___herself___ by going to a movie with her best friend.
2. What happened to his finger? Did he cut _____?
3. Even though I had a bad headache, I forced _____ to study hard.
4. Sarah and Olivia love math, and they challenge _____ to always learn more.
5. When we were little, my brother and I used to pretend we were astronauts. We called _____ "The Moon Boys."

**3. Circle the correct answers.**

1. When I decided to start exercising before school each morning, the first thing I did was ____.
   a. get fixed my alarm clock
   b. (have my alarm clock fixed)
2. Charles won a silver medal in the Olympics. When he came home, he ____.
   a. got it framed
   b. have framed it
3. Jada accidentally stepped on her cell phone and needed to ____.
   a. repair
   b. get it repaired
4. When are you going to ____? You need to do it soon, I think.
   a. take your passport picture
   b. get your passport picture taken
5. When my sister graduated from high school, my parents had a big party for her. They ____.
   a. had a big chocolate cake made
   b. make a big chocolate cake

## Useful language

**4. Complete the conversation.**

| I'm sure | I think I can | worry about it | you've faced |
|---|---|---|---|

**Matt:** Dad, I'm really nervous. I want to try out for the basketball team tomorrow, but I've never played basketball except out in the driveway with you!

**Dad:** ¹_____ you'll do fine. Science nerds can play sports too, you know.

**Matt:** I don't know. I'm tall, but I'm not as tall as some of those guys. And they're all really good.

**Dad:** Basketball isn't all about height. Try not to ²_____ and just do your best.

**Matt:** Don't worry? That's all I do. I don't think I can do this.

**Dad:** Listen, ³_____ bigger challenges than this. Remember last year's science fair? That was harder than basketball tryouts.

**Matt:** No, I don't think so. I'm good at science.

**Dad:** ⁴_____ help you. Let's go outside and practice together.

**Matt:** OK. Thanks!

---

**PROGRESS CHECK: Now I can . . .**

- ☐ talk about goals and accomplishments.
- ☐ discuss emotions related to accomplishments.
- ☐ discuss steps toward achieving goals.
- ☐ reassure someone.
- ☐ write a personal action plan.
- ☐ discuss an academic competition.

## Uncover Your Knowledge
# UNITS 6–10 Review Game

### TEAM 1
### START

- Imagine you have a chance to meet a celebrity, living or dead. Use the second conditional to tell your teammate who you would meet and what you would do.

- Name five things that can happen in school.

- Think of two imaginary situations and ask your teammate what they would do in those situations.

- Say eight different materials that things can be made from.

- Identify four items in your classroom. Say what two of them are made of and what the other two are used for.

- Imagine that you saw a classmate cheating on a test. Explain the situation to your teammate and ask for advice on what to do about it.

- Tell your teammate how you would design and build an eco-friendly building. What would it be? How it would save energy?

- Ask your teammate two questions in the simple past passive. Use Where, When, How, or Who. Your teammate answers with a simple past passive statement.

- In 30 seconds, say two phrases that use the verb do and two phrases that use the verb make.

- What had you known about extreme weather disasters before this unit? Tell your teammate two things you had known, and two things you hadn't known.

- Tell a teammate that he or she has done something that upset you. Your teammate apologizes.

### INSTRUCTIONS:
- Make teams and choose game pieces.
- Put your game pieces on your team's START.
- Flip a coin to see who goes first.
- Read the first challenge. Can you do it correctly?

    Yes → Continue to the next challenge.

    No → Lose your turn.

The first team to do all of the challenges wins!

## TEAM 2
### START

- GRAMMAR
- VOCABULARY
- USEFUL LANGUAGE

1. Tell a teammate two things you did, one before the other. Use the past perfect and simple past.
2. Role-play a conversation with your teammate. Tell them about a personal problem, and have them try to help you.
3. What three items would you want to have if you were lost in the woods? Explain why.
4. Report to your teammate three different things you heard people say yesterday.
5. How do you feel when you are getting ready for a big test? How do you feel when the test is over and you did well? Use at least four emotion words.
6. In 30 seconds, say three sentences that use reflexive pronouns.
7. Name at least one natural disaster that can occur in each area: forests, mountains, tropical islands, and flat areas.
8. Say three phrases you can use to reassure someone.
9. Have your teammate ask you a question. Then tell another teammate what your first teammate asked you.
10. Give six examples of verbs you can use to report speech in 30 seconds.
11. Role-play a conversation with your teammate. Say that something happened to a celebrity last night. Your teammate heard a different version of the story. Compare your stories.
12. Describe a goal you have achieved. Tell your teammate what your goal was, what challenges you faced, and how you dealt with them.
13. Use causative *have/get* to tell your teammate three things that other people do for you.
14. List all the different ways you communicated with people this week.

Units 6–10 Review | 105

This page intentionally left blank.

## Second conditional, page 57

Use the second conditional to describe imaginary situations and possible consequences.

| Imaginary situation | Possible consequences |
|---|---|
| *if* + simple past | *would (not)* + base form of the verb |
| **If** I **changed** the school rules, | students **wouldn't wear** uniforms. |
| **If** you **missed** class, | you **would be** assigned to detention. |
| **If** she **didn't** like the class, | she **wouldn't go**. |

Many American English speakers use *were* rather than *was* after I, he, she, *and* it, especially in a more formal style.

| Formal style | Informal style |
|---|---|
| If I **were** rude to my teacher, my parents would be very mad at me. | If I **was** always punctual, I wouldn't be assigned to detention so much. |

The *if* clause can come at the beginning or end of the sentence. If it's at the beginning, it's followed by a comma.

**If** you missed class**,** she would be assigned to detention.

You would be assigned to detention **if** you missed class.

**1. Write second conditional sentences.**

1. If / you / break / the rules / you / be sent / to the principal's office

   _____

2. If / Sara / not wear / her uniform / she / be assigned / to detention

   _____

3. Carl / not get / extra credit / if / he / cheat / on the assignment

   _____

4. We / be / in trouble / if / we / bully / students

   _____

## Second conditional *Wh-* questions, page 59

Use Wh- questions in the second conditional to ask about imaginary situations and possible consequences.

| What | would your teacher do | if | one of your classmates **cheated** on a test? |
|---|---|---|---|
| Who | would you talk to | if | you **had** a serious problem with a friend? |
| When | would you go to school | if | you **chose** the days you went? |
| If | you wanted to do something fun this weekend, | where | would you **go**? |
| If | you got a new pet, | why | would you **choose** one kind of pet over another? |

**2. Complete the second conditional questions with *what*, *who*, *when*, or *where* and the words in parentheses. Use each question word once.**

1. _____ (you / do) if _____ (you / have) a difficult test to study for?

2. If _____ (Sheri / go) to New York, _____ (she / go)? In the summer?

3. If _____ (you / have) a party, _____ (it / be)? At a restaurant or at your house?

4. _____ (you / ask) for help if _____ (you / not understand) your homework? Your teacher or your friend?

## Simple present passive, page 67

*Use the passive when it is not important who does the action, or when you don't know who does it.*

*To form the simple present passive, use is/are + past participle.*

| Active | Passive |
|---|---|
| **Affirmative** | |
| They **make** this wall of bottles. | This wall **is made** of bottles. |
| People **use** car tires to build strong walls. | Car tires **are used** to build strong walls. |
| **Negative** | |
| They **don't make** that bottle of plastic. | That bottle **isn't made** of plastic. |
| People **don't build** the houses with bricks. | The houses **aren't built** with bricks. |

1. **Complete the sentences in the simple present passive with the verbs from the box.**

   | call | make | not build | not grow | recycle |

   1. The blocks _____ of cement.
   2. This cotton _____ in cold places.
   3. Those plastic bottles _____ to make furniture.
   4. These houses _____ quickly. It takes a long time.
   5. The new exhibit at the museum _____ "Reused Art."

## Simple past passive, page 69

*Use the passive when it is not important who did the action, or when you don't know who did it.*

*To form the simple past passive, use was/were + past participle.*

| Active | Passive |
|---|---|
| **Affirmative** | |
| We **built** the EcoHouse in 1985. | The EcoHouse **was built** in 1985. |
| We **updated** the appliances two months ago. | The appliances **were updated** two months ago. |
| **Negative** | |
| We **didn't install** a recycling bin until last year. | A recycling bin **wasn't installed** until last year. |
| They **didn't install** solar panels 60 years ago. | Solar panels **weren't installed** 60 years ago. |
| *Use by with the passive to show who did the action.* | |
| The EcoHouse **was designed by** the museum. | |
| The most energy **was consumed by** the heater. | |
| *Questions and answers with the passive* | |
| When **was** the EcoHouse **built**? | It **was built** in 1985. |
| **Was** the EcoHouse **built** in 1985? | Yes, it **was**. |
| **Were** the old apartments **destroyed** this year? | No, they **weren't**. |

2. **Complete the conversations with the simple past passive.**

   1. **A:** _____ the program _____ (install) on your computer?
      **B:** Yes, it _____. It _____ (do) yesterday by the computer tech.
   2. **A:** Where _____ the pottery _____ (discover)?
      **B:** It _____ (find) in a pyramid. Then it _____ (take) to a lab by an archeologist. It _____ (not put) in a museum.
   3. **A:** _____ the houses _____ (build) in the 1990s?
      **B:** No, they _____. They _____ (made) in the 1980s.

## Past perfect, page 77

> Use the past perfect to refer to something that happened before a specific time in the past. To form the past perfect, use **had** + past participle.

| Affirmative | Negative |
| --- | --- |
| I/You/He/She/We/They **had read** a book about it. | I/You/He/She/We/They **hadn't heard** about it before then. |
| I/You/He/She/It/We/They **had been** fairly quiet for several years. | I/You/He/She/It/We/They **hadn't been** there before. |
| What **had** I/you/he/she/we/they **heard** about volcanoes before? | |
| Why **hadn't** I/you/he/she/we/they **researched** anything about Indonesia before? | |
| **Contractions**   had = **'d**     had not = **hadn't** | |

**1. Write sentences and questions in the past perfect.**

1. Carolina / hear / about the tornado before her parents / .
   _____

2. what / you / learn / tsunamis before class / ?
   _____

3. Tyler / not read / about the forest fires before / .
   _____

4. they / flown / out of the city before the earthquake / .
   _____

5. why / you / not bring / your bike inside before the hurricane / ?
   _____

## Past perfect and simple past, page 79

> The young man's parents **called** the police after he **had been** gone for three days.
> The boy **had drunk** the liquid from all the contact lens cases when they **found** him.
> The boy **didn't tell** his story until he **had drunk** a lot of water.
>
> 1. We **can** use the past perfect and the simple past in the same sentence.
> 2. We use the **past perfect** for the action that was completed first.

**2. Write sentences with the information in the chart. Use the past perfect and the simple past and the words in parentheses.**

| First Activity | Second Activity |
| --- | --- |
| 1. they put on sunscreen | they go to the beach |
| 2. I not buy a sleeping bag | my friend ask me to go camping |
| 3. she cut her arm | she find the first-aid kit |
| 4. we get lost | we not look at the map |
| 5. he not find his flashlight | the lights went out |

1. (before) _____
2. (when) _____
3. (after) _____
4. (until) _____
5. (before) _____

Unit 8 | 113

## Quoted speech vs. reported speech, page 87

*Use reported speech to tell others what another person said.*

| | Quoted speech | Reported speech |
|---|---|---|
| Simple present | "It **isn't** right," she said. | She said that it **wasn't** right. |
| Simple past | "We **spent** the whole day together," she told me. | She told me that they **had spent** the whole day together. |
| Present perfect | "We**'ve had** a cell phone for 12 years," he said. | They said that they **had had** a cell phone for 12 years. |
| Future with *will* | "I**'ll text** you when I get to the party," he promised. | He promised that he **would text** me when he got to the party. |
| *can* | "I **can send** you an email," she whispered. | She whispered that she **could send** him an email. |
| Present continuous | "I**'m texting** my friends," he explained. | He explained that he **was texting** his friends. |
| Past continuous | "I **was checking** my email," she said. | She said that she **had been checking** her email. |

**1. Read the quoted speech. Then circle the correct answer in the reported speech.**

1. "I'll clean my room tomorrow." Leo said that he **could clean** / **would clean** his room tomorrow.
2. "I didn't do my homework." Todd explained that he **hadn't done** / **wouldn't do** his homework.
3. "I'm terrified of earthquakes." Julie announced that she **was** / **will be** terrified of earthquakes.
4. "I can help you." My sister promised me that she **helped** / **could help** me.

## Reported questions, page 89

*In reported questions, the verbs usually change tenses as in reported speech. The word order in reported questions is the same as in an affirmative sentence.*

| Direct speech questions | Reported questions |
|---|---|
| "Why **do** you **have** makeup on?" | He asked her why she **had** makeup on. |
| "Which blog post **did** you **read**?" | She asked me which blog post I **had read**. |
| "How **have** you **been**?" | He asked me how I **had been**. |
| "When **will** you **chat** with me?" | She asked me when I **would chat** with her. |
| "Who **can help** them send a text message?" | He asked who **could help** them send a text message. |
| "What **are** you **doing**?" | He asked me what I **was doing**. |
| "Where **were** you **going**?" | She asked me where I **had been going**. |
| *Use* **if** *in Yes/No reported questions.* | |
| "Are you on your way?" | He asked **if** we were on our way. |
| "Did you see what happened?" | She asked **if** I had seen what happened. |

**2. Put the words in the correct order to make reported questions.**

1. why / she sent her / Yolanda / so many text messages / asked Maria

   _____

2. asked / I / if / my friend / on my blog post / he would comment

   _____

3. forum / asked Sue / which / she had joined / Lorenzo

   _____

Unit 9

# Reflexive pronouns, page 97

> *Use a reflexive pronoun when an object refers to the subject.*
> **I** like to challenge **myself** by measuring my progress every week.
> **You** need to set a deadline for **yourself**.
> All of **you** should challenge **yourselves** at this job.
> **He** wasn't pleased with **himself** when he heard criticism of his performance.
> **She** taught **herself** the skills she needed to write essays.
> **We** decided to enjoy **ourselves** only after we had studied for the test.
> **Teenagers** can help **themselves** to any of the career planning books we have.
> Many people achieve the goals **they** set for **themselves**.
> An education is important, and **it** can pay for **itself** if you get a good job.

**1. Circle the correct answers.**

1. Maria taught **herself** / **myself** / **himself** to play the piano.
2. You should reward **ourselves** / **yourself** / **myself** for your hard work.
3. My parents usually deal with their problems **yourself** / **themselves** / **ourselves**.
4. Please don't help me. I want to do it by **myself** / **herself** / **yourself**.
5. Liz and I are very pleased with **herself** / **themselves** / **ourselves**.
6. Will Eddie teach **myself** / **himself** / **yourself** the computer skills he needs?

# Causative *have/get*, page 99

> *Use causative* have/get *in situations where someone else does something for you. You don't do it.*
> *You can use* get *or* have. *They have similar meanings.*

|  | have/get | object | past participle |  |
|---|---|---|---|---|
| Lauren | is **getting** | her knee | **examined** | now. |
| Jennifer | **had** | a cake | **made** | for her friend. |
| David | needs to **get** | his camera | **fixed**. |  |
| Logan | will **have** | his eyes | **checked**. |  |

**2. Write sentences about what Sandy did yesterday and what she will do tomorrow.**

| Yesterday | Tomorrow |
|---|---|
| have / tablet / fix | have / hair / cut |
| get / clothes / clean | get / elbow / examine |
| get / homework / check | have / bike / repair |

1. *Sandy* _____
2. *She* _____
3. _____
4. _____
5. _____
6. _____

This page intentionally left blank.

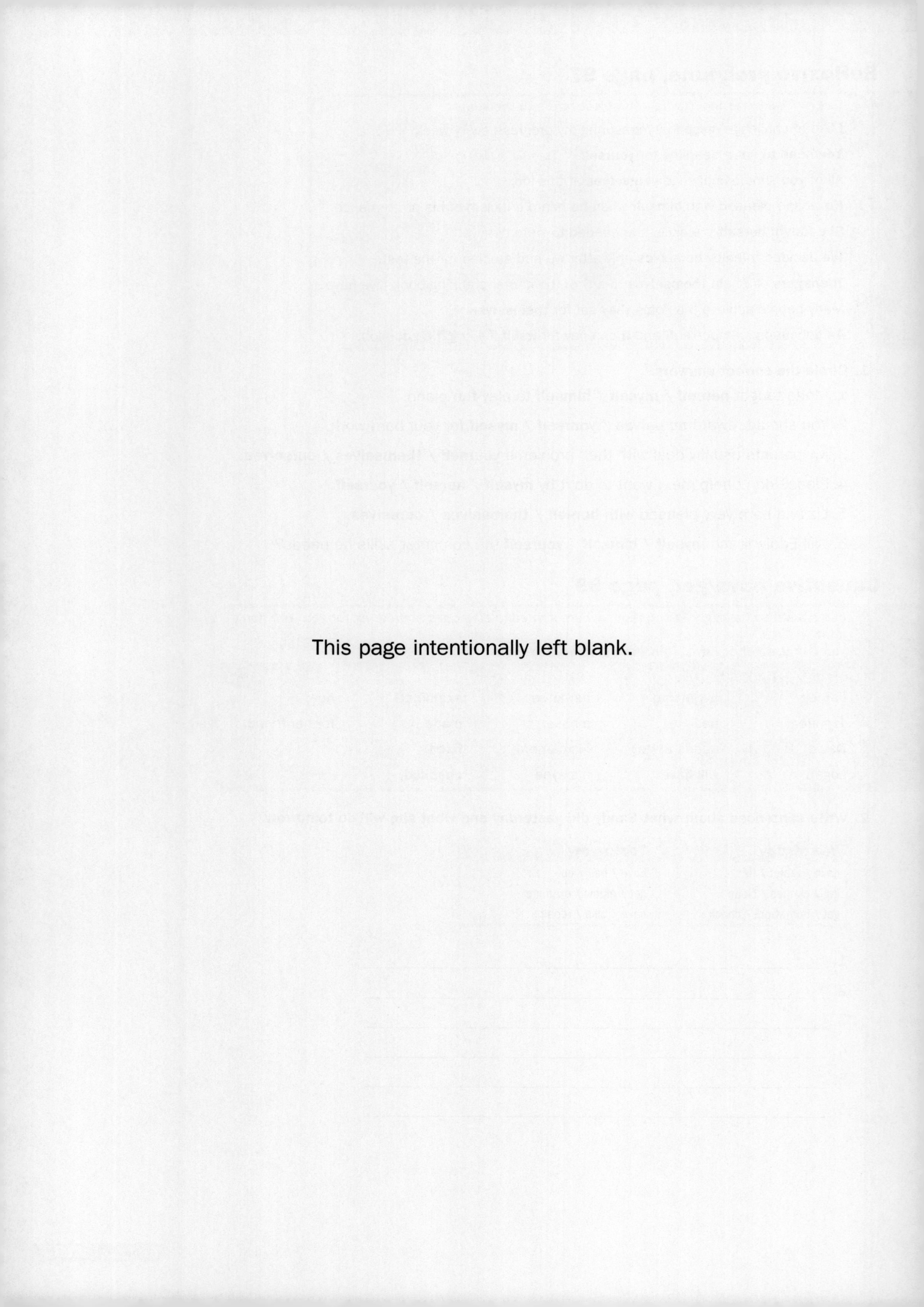

# Rethinking the CAR

1. **Match the words with the correct definitions.**

   1. _____ fossil fuel
   2. _____ carbon dioxide
   3. _____ the environment
   4. _____ battery
   5. _____ renewable energy
   6. _____ solar power

   a. electricity that comes from the sun's heat
   b. energy that comes from the sun, water, or wind
   c. fuel from under the ground, like gas, coal, and oil
   d. it gives energy to make radios, cars, and toys work
   e. the air, water, or land where people, animals, and plants live
   f. we produce this gas when we burn things or when we breathe out

2. **Watch the video. Complete the sentences with the correct words.**

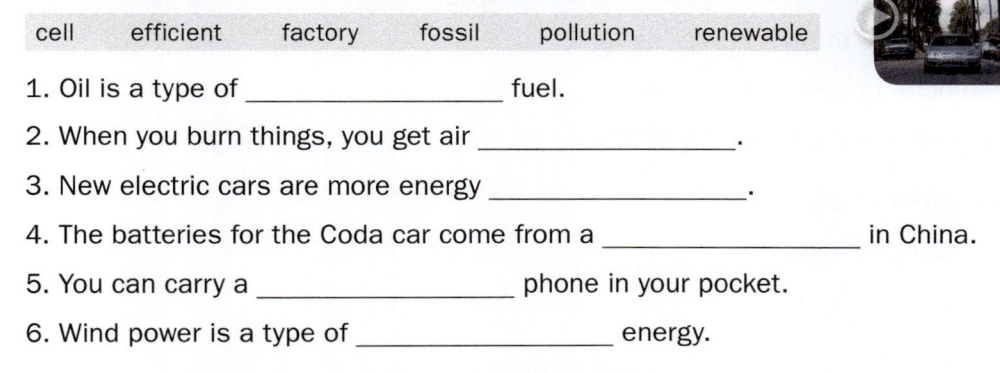

   | cell | efficient | factory | fossil | pollution | renewable |

   1. Oil is a type of _____ fuel.
   2. When you burn things, you get air _____.
   3. New electric cars are more energy _____.
   4. The batteries for the Coda car come from a _____ in China.
   5. You can carry a _____ phone in your pocket.
   6. Wind power is a type of _____ energy.

   **7.4 DRIVING INTO THE FUTURE**

3. **Match the countries 1–4 with the car companies a–d.**

   1. _____ China
   2. _____ Germany
   3. _____ Japan
   4. _____ USA

   a. BMW
   b. Chevy & Ford
   c. BYD
   d. Nissan

**PROJECT**

In groups, think of ways you and your classmates can help the environment. Here are some ideas:

- Recycle your old computers and cell phones
- Save energy in your home (turn off lights when you leave the room, take a two-minute shower, unplug appliances when you're not using them)
- Join an environmental group
- Take the bus, ride a bike, or walk to school

**Make a presentation and show your ideas to the others in the class. Then ask the class to vote on the best ideas.**

# Ancient SYMBOLS

**CLIL PROJECT**

1. **Match the words with the correct definitions.**

   | archeologist | hieroglyphics | skeleton | strap | tomb |

   1. The bones of a human or animal body _____
   2. A person who studies very old places and things _____
   3. Egyptian writing from thousands of years ago _____
   4. A stone structure for a dead body of a person _____
   5. A narrow piece of leather or other strong material. You use it to connect something, like a sandal _____

   **Discovery EDUCATION**
   9.4 PICTURES WITH MEANING

2. **Watch the video. Number the sentences 1–5 in the order that you hear them.**

   a. Mansour Bourek is an archeologist. ____
   b. And here's a goose, a leaf, a mouth, and a strap from a sandal. ____
   c. His team of archeologists come to work inside the tomb. ____
   d. This skeleton has been here for over 2,000 years. ____
   e. Ahmed's family lives above one of the biggest tombs. ____

3. **Match the words with the correct hieroglyphics.**

   | goose | hill country | sun | to cry |

   1 _____   2 _____   3 _____   4 _____

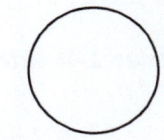

**PROJECT**

About 200 years ago, French soldiers discovered an ancient stone in Egypt with a story written on it. Scientists determined that the story was in three different languages: Greek, Demotic script (the common writing used in ancient Egyptian documents), and in hieroglyphics. The scientists knew how to read Greek, so they were able to understand the hieroglyphics! They named the stone the Rosetta Stone.

Now create your own Rosetta Stone. Write a story about what you think life was like in ancient Egypt. Do research and see if you can translate your story into hieroglyphics.

# Uncover 3 Combo B
## Kathryn O'Dell

## Workbook

CAMBRIDGE UNIVERSITY PRESS

Discovery EDUCATION

# 6 Difficult Decisions

## VOCABULARY  School life

**1 Complete the sentences and the crossword.**

### ACROSS

4. I don't mind wearing a ___uniform___ to school.
7. Many students aren't following the dress _____.
8. We're trying to win a _____ for "best project."
10. Sara was assigned to _____ for being late.

### DOWN

1. Jack got sent to the principal's _____ for talking in class.
2. _____ is not allowed at our school. We must be kind to each other.
3. Tim was caught _____ on a test.
5. I'm getting extra _____ in my English class.
6. I'm always _____. I'm never late for class.
9. Our teacher talked to us about not being _____. She said we have to be more polite.

**2 Complete the paragraph with the correct words or phrases.**

| be assigned | cheating |
| be punctual | follow |
| ✓ be rude | get sent |
| bullying | wear |

### Hampton High School RULES

Do not ¹ ___be rude___ to teachers or other students. ² _____ is not allowed. Students must treat each other kindly. Students who are disrespectful will ³ _____ to the principal's office.

You must ⁴ _____. If you are late more than three times in one month, you'll ⁵ _____ to detention.

There is absolutely no ⁶ _____. Students must do their own work.

All students must ⁷ _____ the dress code. You have to ⁸ _____ school uniforms.

**3 Answer the questions with your own information.**

1. Does your school have a dress code? Do you have to wear school uniforms?

   _Our school has a dress code. Everyone has_
   _to wear a white shirt and black pants._

2. Why do students at your school get sent to the principal's office? Why are they assigned to detention?

   _____
   _____

3. Do you ever get extra credit in your classes? Which classes?

   _____
   _____

## GRAMMAR  Second conditional

**1 Correct the second conditional sentences.**

1. If I ~~would change~~ *changed* our school's dress code, I'd let students wear jeans every day.

2. If you bullied a student, you be assigned to detention.

3. If Sara does the best in the contest, she'd win the prize.

4. If we wasn't punctual, our teacher would be upset.

5. My teacher sends me to the principal's office if I broke the school rules.

6. Luke wouldn't pass the test if he not study.

7. Debbie would tell the teacher if she would see someone cheating.

8. I'd go to the soccer game I didn't have to study.

**2 Complete the paragraph with the second conditional.**

If Tim ¹ *bullied* (bully) students, he ² _____ (be) assigned to detention. If he ³ _____ (be) assigned to detention, his parents ⁴ _____ (be) angry. If his parents ⁵ _____ (be) angry, they ⁶ _____ (make) him do chores. If Tim ⁷ _____ (have) to do chores, he ⁸ _____ (not be) happy. Tim had better not bully students!

**3 Write second conditional sentences with the information in the chart.**

| | Imaginary situation | Possible consequence |
|---|---|---|
| 1. | Leo / fail / his test | his parents / be / angry |
| 2. | You / not call me | I / wonder / why |
| 3. | Carla / win / the prize | she / be / happy |
| 4. | Mark and Doug / not have / class | they / go / to the concert |
| 5. | Jenny / go / on vacation | she / miss / her classes |
| 6. | I / be rude / to my classmates | I / get sent / to the principal's office |

1. *If Leo failed his test, his parents would be angry.*
2. _____
3. _____
4. _____
5. _____
6. _____

## Second conditional yes/no questions

**4 Write second conditional questions. Then answer the questions with your own information.**

1. if / your friends / go / to a concert / your parents / let / you go with them

   Q: *If your friends went to a concert, would your parents let you go with them?*

   A: *Yes, they would.* OR *No, they wouldn't.*

2. if / your friend / bully / another student / you / tell / the principal

   Q: _____
   A: _____

3. you / apologize / if / you / be / rude to a classmate

   Q: _____
   A: _____

4. your parents / be / angry / if / you / cheat / on a test

   Q: _____
   A: _____

## VOCABULARY  Expressions with *make* and *do*

**1** Write the expressions in the correct places in the chart. Add *make* or *do*.

| a difference | research |
| friends | something fun |
| ✓ homework | the right thing |
| me a favor | you mad |

| do | make |
|---|---|
| do homework | _____ |
| _____ | _____ |
| _____ | _____ |
| _____ | _____ |

**2** Complete the sentences with the correct expressions from Exercise 1.

1. Jacob likes to __do the right thing__ at school. He always follows the rules.
2. Charlotte is very friendly, and it's easy for her to _____.
3. Kyle really wants to _____ at his school. He started a "stop bullying" group.
4. I want to _____ this weekend. Let's go sailing!
5. Can you _____? I need help with my homework.
6. I never want to _____. I don't like it when you're angry.
7. My sister likes to _____ for school projects. She loves learning new things.
8. I can't go to the park. I have to _____.

**3** Circle the correct words. Then write answers with your own information.

1. How often do you **do** / **make** homework? Where do you **do** / **make** it?
   _I do homework every night. I do it at my desk._
2. Have you ever **done** / **made** a favor for someone? What did you **do** / **make**?
   _____
   _____
3. Do you **do** / **make** research online? When?
   _____
   _____
4. When do you **do** / **make** something fun? What do you **do** / **make**?
   _____
   _____
5. Do you **do** / **make** friends easily? How do you **do** / **make** new friends?
   _____
   _____
6. When your friends break the rules, do you **do** / **make** the right thing? What do you **do** / **make**?
   _____
   _____
7. Who **does** / **makes** you mad? Why?
   _____
   _____
8. Have you ever **done** / **made** a difference at your school? What was it?
   _____
   _____

## GRAMMAR  Second conditional Wh- questions

**1 Match the questions with the answers.**

| | |
|---|---|
| 1. What would you do if you didn't finish your homework? _d_ | a. I'd go in August. |
| 2. Who would you tell if someone bullied you at school? ___ | b. I'd make new friends. |
| 3. How would you do research if you had to write a paper? ___ | c. I'd find information online. |
| 4. If you went on vacation, when would you go? ___ | d. I'd ask my teacher for more time. |
| 5. If your friend was rude to you, what would you say? ___ | e. I'd tell the principal. |
| 6. What would you do if your family moved to a new city? ___ | f. I'd tell her I was upset. |

**2 Circle the correct words.**

**Anna:** Hey, David. What ¹**did / would** you do if your friend ²**asked / would ask** you to cheat on a test?

**David:** I'd say no! I'd never do that.

**Anna:** So, if your friend ³**cheated / would cheat**, who ⁴**did / would** you tell?

**David:** Hmm. I probably wouldn't tell anyone.

**Anna:** Really? Why ⁵**wouldn't / didn't** you tell anyone if your friend ⁶**did / would do** something wrong?

**David:** Well, I'd try to get my friend to do the right thing and tell someone.

**Anna:** That's a good idea.

**3 Write the questions another way. Then answer the questions with your own information.**

1. Where would you study if you had a test tomorrow?

   Q: _If you had a test tomorrow, where would you study?_

   A: _I'd study at the café._

2. If you broke your friend's computer, what would you do?

   Q: _____
   A: _____

3. If you did someone a favor, who would you help?

   Q: _____
   A: _____

4. Where would you celebrate if you had a party for your birthday?

   Q: _____
   A: _____

5. What would you do if you didn't have homework tonight?

   Q: _____
   A: _____

**4 Complete the questions. Use the pictures and answers to help you.**

1. Q: What _would Tony do if it rained_?

   A: He'd take an umbrella.

2. Q: Where _____?

   A: They'd go rafting in Costa Rica.

3. Q: _____

   A: She'd apologize to the teacher.

## CONVERSATION — Asking for and giving advice

**1** Put the words in the correct order.

1. on / what's / going / ?
   *What's going on?*

2. advice / need / some / I / .
   _____

3. up / what's / sure / . / ?
   _____

4. do / what / I / should / ?
   _____

5. ask him / I / in person / you, / I'd / if / were / .
   _____

6. for it / you / asking him / have / tried / ?
   _____

**2** Complete the conversation with the phrases from Exercise 1.

**Haley:** Hi, Brian. You look upset.
¹ *What's going on?*

**Brian:** Well, I'm really mad at Peter. I don't know what to do.
² _____

**Haley:** ³ _____

**Brian:** Well, Peter borrowed my tablet last week, and he hasn't given it back.
⁴ _____

**Haley:** ⁵ _____

**Brian:** Yes, I have. I sent him three text messages about it.

**Haley:** You know, maybe he didn't read the texts.
⁶ _____

**Brian:** Well, I guess that's a good idea.

**Haley:** Yeah. You might be getting mad for no good reason!

**Brian:** You're probably right. I'll go talk to him!

# READING TO WRITE

**1 Complete the article with the imperative form of the verbs.**

| be | invite | not wait |
|---|---|---|
| ✓ follow | join | remember |
| go | not be | |

## HOW TO MAKE FRIENDS

It can be difficult to make friends, especially if you move to a new city. So, how can you make friends easily?

¹ _____Follow_____ this advice.

² _____ places where there are a lot of teens. For example, go to a café or the library.

³ _____ a club. Do you like chess, sports, or photography? Find a club with your interests.

Find friends online with similar interests. But ⁴ _____ careful when you make friends online. Some people can be bullies online.

⁵ _____ to be friendly and smile when you meet new people. ⁶ _____ afraid to say hello and ask questions. ⁷ _____ for others to talk to you. You can be the one to start a conversation!

Stay in touch with new friends. Call, text, or email them.

⁸ _____ new friends to do things.

**2 Read the article in Exercise 1 again. Circle the correct answers.**

1. What's the title?
   a. Moving to a New City
   b. How to Make Friends
   c. Follow This Advice

2. What's the problem?
   a. Some people can be bullies online.
   b. It's hard to stay in touch with friends.
   c. It's sometimes hard to make friends.

3. Who does this problem affect?
   a. People who have moved to a new city.
   b. Teenagers who don't have any friends.
   c. People who want to make friends online.

4. What question does the article want to answer?
   a. Do you like making friends?
   b. How can you make friends easily?
   c. Why is it difficult to make friends?

**3 Complete the article with the correct sentences.**

Choose your friends carefully.
Don't be afraid to tell your friends they are wrong.
Get away from the situation.
✓ How can you avoid peer pressure?
Say "no" and mean it.

## How to Avoid PEER PRESSURE

Peer pressure is when your friends try to make you do things that they are doing. Sometimes, they might not be doing the right thing.

¹ _____How can you avoid peer pressure?_____
Follow this advice.

² _____

It's important to be strong if you don't want to do something. You might have to say "no" more than once.

³ _____

If you walk away from something you don't want to do, your friends can't make you do it.

⁴ _____

Hang out with friends that make good decisions.

⁵ _____

They may listen to you and decide to do the right thing.

# REVIEW UNITS 5–6

**1** Complete each sentence with a word or phrase from each box.

| confused | bullying |
|---|---|
| embarrassing | clowns |
| interesting | ✓ did me a favor |
| ✓ surprised | do research |
| terrified | snakes |
| terrifying | wear a school uniform |

1. I was ___surprised___ when Rick ___did me a favor___. He never wants to help me.
2. I was _____ when the girls at school started _____ me. They were saying very mean things, and I was scared.
3. I think _____ are _____. I always scream when I see one outside in my yard.
4. I have to _____. I have to keep it on for my piano lesson because I don't have time to change. It's so _____!
5. I think it's _____ to _____. I love finding out about new things.
6. I'm _____. Sarah said she was afraid of _____, but she's posting pictures of them at the circus. It looks like she's having a good time.

**2** Write the words in the correct places in the chart.

| ✓ elevators | relaxed |
|---|---|
| exhausted | the dark |
| getting extra credit | winning an award |

| Fears | elevators | |
|---|---|---|
| Feelings | | |
| Rewards | | |

**3** Complete the expressions with *do* or *make*.

1. ___do___ something fun
2. _____ me mad
3. _____ homework
4. _____ a difference
5. _____ friends

**4** Look at the pictures. Complete the sentences with *be going to* and an expression from Exercise 3.

1. Isabel *is going to do something fun* this weekend.
2. Amy and Dan _____ at their new school. 
3. You _____ if you don't clean your room. 
4. Jeremy _____ after school. 
5. I _____ in my community by helping others. 

**5** Circle the correct words.

1. Oh, no, you forgot to do your homework. You **can't** / (**must**) be really (**embarrassed**) / **embarrassing**.
2. This math problem is very **confused** / **confusing**. I think I **might** / **can't** have the wrong answer.
3. Ginger's vacation is **relaxed** / **relaxing**. She **may** / **might not** want to stay a few more days.
4. I'm **interested** / **interesting** in being a police officer, but it **must** / **must not** be very difficult.
5. Jen told me **surprised** / **surprising** news. She won an award. She **can't** / **might** be sad about that!
6. The race is going to be **exhausted** / **exhausting**. It **can't** / **could** take me an hour or more to finish.

**6** Complete the conversations. Use *will* for decisions at the moment of speaking. Use the present continuous for planned events.

1. **A:** Do you want to go to a theme park this weekend?
   **B:** Sure. I _____'ll go_____ (go) with you.
2. **A:** What are you going to do tomorrow?
   **B:** I _____ (shop) with my sister.
3. **A:** When are you going to Lima?
   **B:** We _____ (fly) there tomorrow.
4. **A:** Do you have homework tonight?
   **B:** I _____ (not know) until after my next class.
5. **A:** How are you getting home?
   **B:** I'm not sure. I think I _____ (walk).
6. **A:** Where is your brother staying tonight?
   **B:** He _____ (sleep) at my grandparents' house.

**7** Complete the sentences with the correct forms of the verbs.

1. If Jim didn't stay up so late, he ____wouldn't feel____ (not feel) exhausted in the morning.
2. If Sara misses class again, she _____ (be) assigned detention.
3. If you _____ (not follow) the dress code, you'll be sent home.
4. If your best friend cheated on a test, what _____ you _____ (do)?
5. If Noah _____ (not be) rude, he wouldn't have to apologize.
6. If your classmates saw someone being bullied, _____ they _____ (tell) the teacher?
7. If you cheat on the test, you _____ (get) sent to the principal's office.
8. If you _____ (win) a prize, how would you feel?
9. If you are punctual, you _____ (not make) Mr. Gomez mad.
10. If you _____ (be) late to class, would you be embarrassed?

**8** Complete the conversation.

| Have you tried talking to him? | Come on! |
| Are you serious? | ✓ I need some advice. |
| Sure. What's up? | What should I do? |

**Julia:** Hey, Ryan.
¹ *I need some advice.*

**Ryan:** ² _____

**Julia:** Well, did you hear about Aaron? He was assigned to detention.

**Ryan:** ³ _____

**Julia:** Yes, I am. And he's not going to tell our parents.

**Ryan:** ⁴ _____
That doesn't sound like your brother.

**Julia:** I know.
⁵ _____

**Ryan:** ⁶ _____
You could tell him this: If he tells your parents before the principal does, it probably won't make them as mad.

**Julia:** That's a good idea.

# 7 Smart Planet

**VOCABULARY** Materials

**1** Find 10 more words for materials.

| M | H | I | T | H | K | W | O | A | M | W | U | B | B | M |
|---|---|---|---|---|---|---|---|---|---|---|---|---|---|---|
| B | A | N | O | Z | O | J | T | L | E | N | N | G | R | P |
| R | U | B | B | E | R | U | I | C | T | U | I | S | P | Z |
| O | A | I | N | V | B | I | Y | B | A | A | Q | N | L | R |
| T | C | C | O | T | T | O | N | N | L | Y | A | T | A | T |
| O | K | E | A | I | L | I | P | L | A | N | T | S | S | I |
| E | P | M | I | Y | C | B | A | S | T | I | D | A | T | K |
| R | B | E | N | R | W | O | O | D | R | B | R | I | I | C |
| A | R | N | B | O | A | M | O | U | N | F | O | M | C | I |
| N | I | T | I | O | T | E | P | L | A | E | N | A | H | R |
| T | C | C | K | N | E | S | A | G | L | A | S | S | E | M |
| G | K | K | I | S | R | S | L | S | I | T | T | O | G | J |
| I | S | D | N | U | S | A | P | A | P | E | R | U | F | L |

**2** Cross out the word that doesn't belong to each category.

1. **Water:** ocean lake ~~mountain~~ river
2. **Wood:** house tablet guitar table
3. **Cement:** floor house road car
4. **Plants:** waterfall jungle rain forest farm
5. **Rubber:** tire T-shirt bath toy balloon
6. **Metal:** fork jewelry book chair
7. **Plastic:** magazine bottle keyboard cup
8. **Glass:** window mirror pottery light bulb

**3** Complete the sentences with some of the materials from Exercise 1.

1. It's a ___cotton___ sweater.
2. I live in a _____ house. 
3. It's a _____ jar. 
4. I made a _____ airplane. 
5. Do you like my new _____ boots? 
6. Put those things in the _____ recycling bin. 
7. _____ flows out of the fountain. 
8. Use some _____ to start the fire. 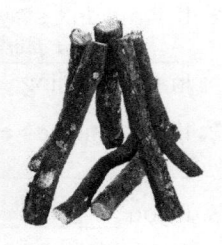

**4** Answer the questions with your own information.

1. What material is in the floors of your home?
   _The floors in my home are wood._
2. What kind of bottle or can do you usually buy soda or juice in?
   _____
3. What kinds of clothes do you wear that are cotton?
   _____
4. What materials can you recycle in your area?
   _____

44 | Unit 7

## GRAMMAR  Simple present passive; infinitives of purpose

**1  Correct the sentences.**

1. My favorite T-shirt ~~are~~ *is* made from cotton.
2. Those cars are built be less harmful to the environment.
3. The animals in the wildlife park isn't hunted.
4. The water on the river not frozen because it's not cold enough.
5. Rubber is used to made erasers.
6. Plastic bottles aren't recycle at our recycling center.
7. These plants grown in a greenhouse.
8. Water isn't sell in plastic bottles at that store.

**2  Write sentences with the simple present passive.**

1. the buildings / design / in California
   *The buildings are designed in California.*
2. the fruit / grow / in Mexico
   _____
3. the cabinets / not make / of wood
   _____
4. the wall / not paint / green
   _____
5. the park / clean / every weekend
   _____
6. the glass bottles / not reused / at the market
   _____

**3  Look at the pictures and answer the questions.**

1. Where is the house built?
   *It's built in a forest.*
2. What is the house made of?
   _____
3. What is recycled at the recycling center? 
   _____
4. What isn't recycled?
   _____
5. Where are the oranges grown? 
   _____
6. Where is the tomato sauce made?
   _____

**4  Write sentences with the information in the chart. Use the simple present passive and infinitives of purpose.**

| What? | Why? |
|---|---|
| those cotton T-shirts / make | keep / people cool |
| that house / design | save / energy |
| plastic bottles / recycle | make / furniture |
| bricks / use | build / houses |
| that wood / save | make / fires |

1. *Those cotton T-shirts are made to keep people cool.*
2. _____
3. _____
4. _____
5. _____

# VOCABULARY  Eco-construction verbs

**1** Circle seven more verbs.

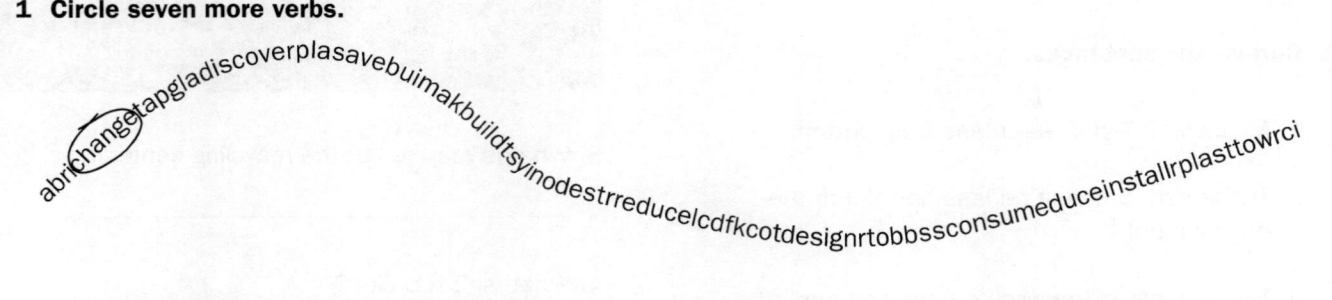

abri(change)tapgladiscoverplasavebuimakbuildtsyinodestrreducelcdfkcotdesignrtobbssconsumeduceinstallrplasttowrci

**2** Put the words in the correct categories. Some words can go in more than one category. Then add one more idea for each category.

| ✓ a house | energy |
|---|---|
| a new plant | pollution |
| an air-conditioning unit | the rain forest |
| clothes | |

| Things you can . . . | | Your ideas |
|---|---|---|
| 1. build | *a house* | |
| 2. change | | |
| 3. install | | |
| 4. reduce | | |
| 5. discover | | |
| 6. design | *a house* | |
| 7. save | | |
| 8. consume | | |

**3** Complete the sentences with the present continuous of the verbs from Exercise 1.

1. Mr. and Mrs. Henderson _are installing_ solar panels on their roof.

2. Jenny _____ money because she _____ her light bulbs to ones that don't use as much energy.

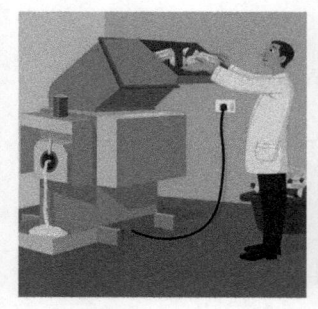

3. Tomás _____ a new way to recycle plastic.

4. Laura _____ a house for her parents.

5. They _____ a house in the city.

6. We _____ trash in our school by 50 percent.

46 | Unit 7

## GRAMMAR  Simple past passive

**1 Check (✓) if the sentences are active or passive.**

|  | Active | Passive |
|---|---|---|
| 1. The houses were built in 2013. |  | ✓ |
| 2. The company installed three recycling bins in the cafeteria. |  |  |
| 3. John's family doesn't grow corn on their farm. |  |  |
| 4. Our windows weren't replaced after the last storm. |  |  |
| 5. Large amounts of fuel were consumed by cars and trucks last year. |  |  |
| 6. Sara designed three new eco-friendly homes this year. |  |  |

**2 Circle the correct words.**

Make your home or business work for you, and let Eco-Friendly Now help you.

Last year, over 100 homes ¹**was made** / **were made** eco-friendly by our company.

Two-hundred and fifty solar panels ²**installed** / **were installed** in local businesses. The businesses ³**saved** / **were saved** thousands of dollars on their electric bills.

A new energy-saving technique ⁴**was developed** / **were developed** by our expert engineer. It ⁵**put** / **was put** in our first home last month.

We ⁶**changed** / **were changed** air conditioning systems in 25 homes, and bills ⁷**reduced** / **were reduced** by 40 percent.

Click here to read reviews that ⁸**was written** / **were written** by happy customers.

**3 Complete the conversation with the simple past passive forms of the verbs.**

Don: Hey, Kim. Are you going to join the School Improvement club?

Kim: What's that?

Don: Oh, it's a group at school that makes changes at our school. Last year, recycling bins ¹ __were put__ (put) in the cafeteria by the group.

Kim: That's cool. What other things ² _____ (do) by the group?

Don: Well, 100 trees ³_____ (plant) around the school.

Eva: ⁴_____ the garden _____ (create) by the group, too?

Don: Yes, it ⁵_____. The garden ⁶_____ (design) by one of the group members.

Eva: ⁷_____ it _____ (design) by Julia Alvarez?

Don: No, it ⁸_____. I think the plans ⁹_____ (draw) by Mark Reynolds. Anyway, it's a great club.

Eva: How many people ¹⁰_____ (involve) in the group last year?

Don: About 10. But we're trying to get at least 25 members this year.

Eva: OK. I'll join!

**4 Write simple past passive sentences and questions. Add *by* when needed.**

1. my dress / make / my grandmother / .
   *My dress was made by my grandmother.*

2. our house / not build / a famous architect / .
   _____

3. the company / start / a designer / ?
   _____

4. those potatoes / not grow / local farmers / .
   _____

5. when / solar panels / invent / ?
   _____

6. the plastic bottles / recycle / the students / .
   _____

7. where / the pottery / find / ?
   _____

8. lights / leave on / the children / ?
   _____

## CONVERSATION  Apologizing

**1  Circle the correct words.**

**Ryan:** This planting project was a great idea.

**Carla:** Yeah. The park is going to look so much better. Hey, Ryan, did you bring shovels for us?

**Ryan:** Oh, no. I forgot. I'm really [1] **sorry / fault**.

**Carla:** Ryan! How are we going to plant our trees? You said you'd bring them.

**Ryan:** I know. I didn't [2] **forget / mean** to leave them at home.

**Carla:** Here comes Ms. Lee.

**Ms. Lee:** Hi, Carla and Ryan. What's going on? The other students have planted a lot of trees already.

**Carla:** My [3] **sorry / apologies**. We forgot our shovels.

**Ryan:** It was my [4] **fault / apologies**, Ms. Lee. I was supposed to bring the shovels, and I forgot.

**Ms. Lee:** Don't worry about it. You can borrow Javier's and Kayla's shovels. They're almost done.

**2  Complete the conversation with the correct words.**

| apologies | fault | mean | sorry |
|---|---|---|---|

**Ana:** Which flowers should we plant first?

**Eric:** Let's plant your flowers, Ana. Then we can plant Meg's. And finally mine. Meg, where are the flowers you brought?

**Meg:** Oh, I didn't bring any flowers. Was I supposed to?

**Eric:** We were all supposed to bring flowers.

**Meg:** Oh, I see. My [1]_____.

**Eric:** Now we don't have enough!

**Meg:** I didn't [2]_____ to mess things up. I didn't know.

**Eric:** Well, the website about the planting project gave all of the information.

**Ana:** Eric, don't get mad at Meg. I invited her at the last minute. It was my [3]_____. I forgot to tell her about the website, and I didn't tell her to bring flowers.

**Eric:** Oh, wow. I'm really [4]_____, Meg.

**Meg:** That's OK. Hey, there's a garden center a few minutes away. I'll go buy some flowers now.

**Eric:** No! I'll go get them, Meg.

**Ana:** Hey, let's plant these flowers first, and then we'll all go!

# READING TO WRITE

**1** Read the article. Then match the words to different words that refer to the same thing.

## Riverdale Teens Have An
## Animal Adoption Day
by Jordan Pierce

Fifteen Riverdale High School students found homes for animals on Saturday, May 6. The teens worked with the Riverdale Animal Shelter to find homes for cats and dogs. They organized an Animal Adoption Day. They got 20 cats and dogs from the shelter and took them to Riverdale Park for the event. They set up a table there with signs and information about the animals.

All 20 animals were adopted by Riverdale families. The shelter was very happy with the results. It is going to continue working with the teenagers and have an Animal Adoption Day once a month.

1. Riverdale High School students __c__, _____, _____
2. animals _____, _____
3. the Riverdale Animal Shelter _____, _____
4. Animal Adoption Day _____
5. Riverdale Park _____

a. cats and dogs
b. the event
c. they
d. it
e. the teens
f. there
g. the teenagers
h. them
i. the shelter

**2** Read the article in Exercise 1 again. Answer the questions.

1. What was the event?
   _The event was an Animal Adoption Day._
2. When was it?
   _____
3. Where was it?
   _____
4. Who was involved?
   _____
5. What did they do?
   _____
6. What were the results?
   _____
7. What will happen next?
   _____

# 8 Run for Cover!

**VOCABULARY** Natural disasters

1 Put the letters in the correct order to make words.

1. ONTROAD — _tornado_
2. DDLLINAES — _____
3. MSATINU — _____
4. RNHUIACER — _____
5. CNCOVLAI — _____
6. ETRFOS — _____
7. OLFOD — _____
8. UATAEQKERH — _____
9. OREPNUIT — _____
10. IFER — _____
11. AACEVALNH — _____

2 Label the pictures with the correct words from Exercise 1.

1. _tornado_
2. _____ 
3. _____ 
4. _____ 
5. _____ 
6. _____ 
7. _____ 
8. _____ 
9. _____ 

3 Where do the natural disasters happen? Write the words in the correct places in the chart. Some words can go in more than one category.

✓ avalanche | forest fire | tornado
earthquake | hurricane | tsunami
flood | landslide | volcanic eruption

| On land | In the air | In the ocean |
|---|---|---|
| avalanche | | |
| | | |
| | | |

4 When do the natural disasters happen? Check (✓) the answers that are true for your area. Then answer the questions.

| | Often | Sometimes | Never |
|---|---|---|---|
| 1. avalanches | | | |
| 2. earthquakes | | | |
| 3. floods | | | |
| 4. forest fires | | | |
| 5. hurricanes | | | |
| 6. landslides | | | |
| 7. tornadoes | | | |
| 8. tsunamis | | | |
| 9. volcanic eruptions | | | |

1. Which natural disasters happen most often in your area?

   _In my area, tornadoes happen most often._
   _____

2. Which natural disasters never happen in your area? Have you ever experienced them in other places?

   _____
   _____

50 | Unit 8

## GRAMMAR  Past perfect

**1 Write the past perfect forms of the verbs.**

1. plan  _had planned_
2. be  _____
3. not be  _____
4. ski  _____
5. not finish  _____
6. not see  _____
7. hear  _____
8. feel  _____

**2 Complete the paragraph with verbs from Exercise 1.**

### Tell us your NATURAL DISASTER STORIES

**Rachel Patterson:**

My family ¹ _had planned_ a trip to Japan. Then we couldn't go because my father got sick. We finally went a year later. We ² _____ there for two days when an earthquake happened. I ³ _____ earthquakes in California before, but never one like this! We were at a restaurant, and I ⁴ _____ my lunch. It went flying across the room!

**David Alba:**

I ⁵ _____ snow before. But last week, I saw a lot of it! I went skiing in Denver, Colorado. I took ski lessons on the first day. My instructor ⁶ _____ all over the world, and she was a great teacher. There ⁷ _____ an avalanche at the ski resort in over 10 years. However, on the second day, my instructor ⁸ _____ on TV that conditions were right for avalanches, so she cancelled our lessons. Later that day, no one was allowed to ski, and there was an avalanche! Luckily, I was safe!

**3 Read the sentences. Then circle the answer that correctly explains each situation.**

1. Elsa hadn't been to Costa Rica before her trip.
   a. She has been to Costa Rica more than once.
   b. She went to Costa Rica once.

2. The forest fire had started before breakfast.
   a. The forest fire started in the morning.
   b. The forest fire started in the afternoon.

3. Andrew had read an interesting article about tsunamis.
   a. Andrew read an article about tsunamis.
   b. Andrew didn't read an article about tsunamis.

4. Sun-hi hadn't told Paul about the hurricane.
   a. Paul knew about the hurricane.
   b. Paul didn't know about the hurricane.

5. June had finished the reading before school.
   a. June finished the reading.
   b. June didn't finish the reading.

6. The weather hadn't been good before the disaster.
   a. The disaster caused the weather to be bad.
   b. The disaster didn't cause the weather to be bad.

## Past perfect yes/no questions

**4 Write yes/no questions and answers in the past perfect. ✓ = yes, ✗ = no.**

1. Dylan / hear / about the volcanic eruption / (✗)
   Q: _Had Dylan heard about the volcanic eruption?_
   A: _No, he hadn't._

2. you / be / to San Francisco before the earthquake / (✓)
   Q: _____
   A: _____

3. Sally / read / the article before class / (✗)
   Q: _____
   A: _____

4. your parents / tell / about the flood / (✗)
   Q: _____
   A: _____

5. the volcano / be / quiet for several months / (✓)
   Q: _____
   A: _____

6. you and your brother / see / a tornado / before / (✓)
   Q: _____
   A: _____

## VOCABULARY Survival essentials

**1 Match the sentences to the pictures.**

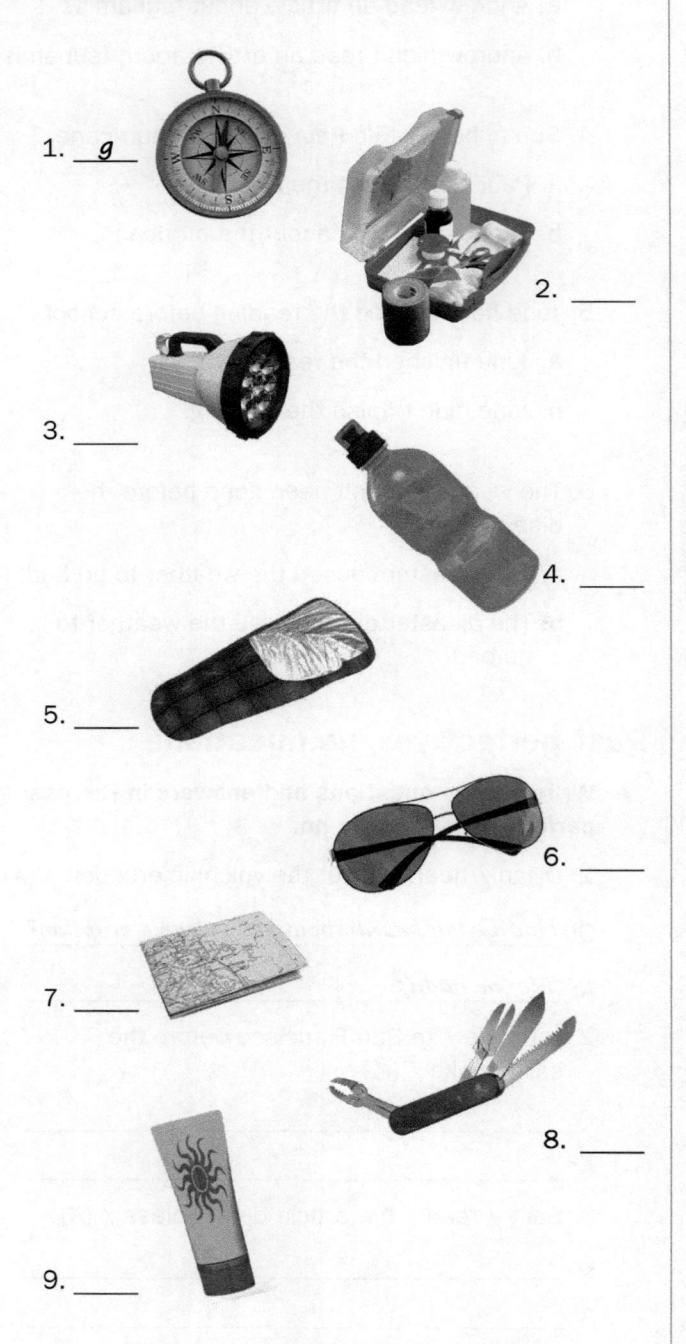

1. _g_
2. ___
3. ___
4. ___
5. ___
6. ___
7. ___
8. ___
9. ___

a. I always take a water bottle when I hike.
b. A penknife is useful on a camping trip.
c. You should wear sunglasses when it's sunny.
d. You should always wear sunscreen outside.
e. I cut my finger. I need a first-aid kit.
f. Your sleeping bag looks really warm.
g. Which way is north? Do you have a compass?
h. I need a flashlight. I'm afraid of the dark!
i. John had forgotten to bring a map on the hike.

**2 Read the situations and circle the correct answers.**

1. Gabriel is skiing in the mountains. It's really bright outside. What does he need?
   a. a compass   b. a first-aid kit   c. sunscreen

2. Carol is lost in a forest. She wants to find her way out before it's dark. What should she use?
   a. a penknife   b. a compass   c. a flashlight

3. Han is camping and sleeping in a tent. What does he need to stay warm?
   a. a flashlight   b. a sleeping bag   c. sunglasses

4. Mara fell and hurt her foot while snowboarding. What does she need?
   a. a water bottle   b. a penknife   c. a first-aid kit

5. Dan and Ethan need to cut a rope on their tent. What should they use?
   a. a penknife   b. sunscreen   c. a first-aid kit

6. Yae-won needs directions to the campgrounds. What should she use?
   a. a sleeping bag   b. a compass   c. a map

**3 Answer the questions with words from Exercise 1.**

1. Which two items protect you from the sun?
   _____
   _____

2. Which two items help you with directions?
   _____
   _____

3. Which two items would you most likely use at night?
   _____
   _____

4. Which two items would you most likely use for food or drink?
   _____
   _____

## GRAMMAR  Past perfect and simple past

**1** Look at the timeline of Carl's trip. Complete the sentences with the past perfect or simple past. Use the past perfect for the event that happened first in each sentence.

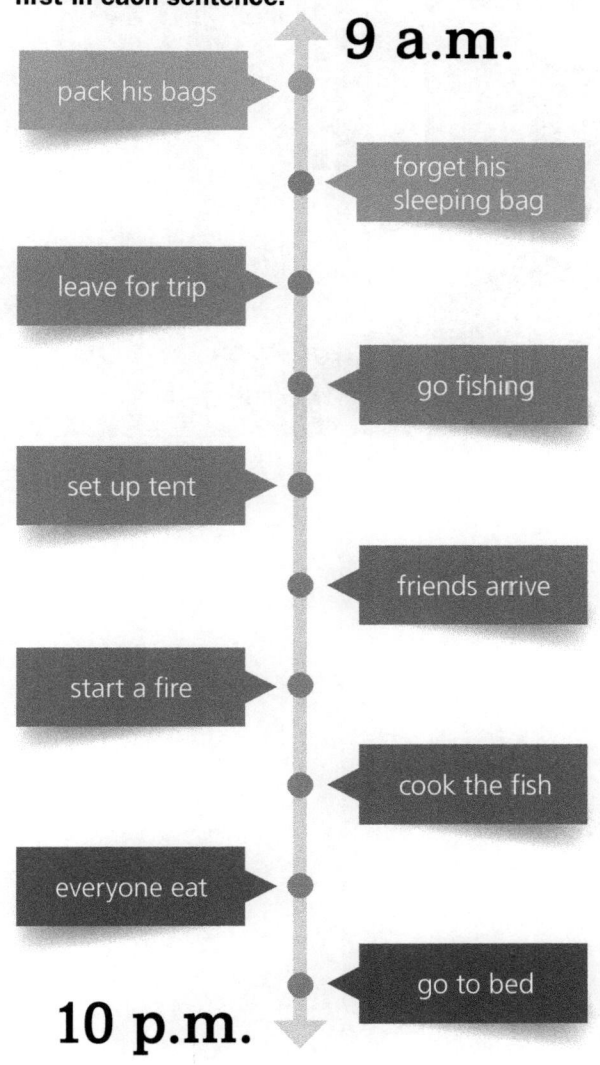

**9 a.m.**
- pack his bags
- forget his sleeping bag
- leave for trip
- go fishing
- set up tent
- friends arrive
- start a fire
- cook the fish
- everyone eat
- go to bed

**10 p.m.**

1. Carl ____had packed____ had packed his bags a week before he ____left____ for his trip.
2. He _____ fishing before he _____ his tent.
3. He _____ his tent already when his friends _____ at the campsite.
4. A few minutes before Carl _____ the fish, he _____ a fire.
5. Everyone _____ a delicious fish dinner a few hours before they _____ to bed.
6. When Carl _____ to bed, he realized that he _____ his sleeping bag!

**2** Circle the correct words. Use the past perfect for the event that happened first in each sentence.

1. On a long hike, John **dropped** / **(had dropped)** his compass 20 minutes before he **(realized)** / **had realized** it.
2. My sister **heard** / **had heard** about the hurricane before I **told** / **had told** her about it.
3. I **cut** / **had cut** my finger making dinner, and unfortunately, I **didn't buy** / **hadn't bought** a first-aid kit.
4. Sam and Jill were hungry on their hike because they **didn't pack** / **hadn't packed** any snacks before they **left** / **had left**.
5. When they **rescued** / **had rescued** the hikers, they **were** / **had been** lost for two days.
6. I was upset because after I **bought** / **had bought** my penknife, the store **had** / **had had** a big sale.

**3** Write sentences with the simple past and past perfect. Use the past perfect for the event that happened first in each sentence.

1. Jessica / sign up / for a camping trip / after / her friend / tell her about it

   *Jessica signed up for the camping trip*
   *after her friend had told her about it.*

2. By the time / Raul / buy / his bike, / he / save / money for two months

   _____
   _____

3. I / not check / the weather report / before / I / go / hiking

   _____
   _____

4. We / pack / our suitcase / a week before / we / leave

   _____
   _____

5. Serena / not hear / about the tsunami / before / she / talk / to her brother

   _____
   _____

6. After / the news / be / on for an hour, / I / finally / hear / the weather report

   _____
   _____

Unit 8 | 53

**CONVERSATION** Asking about and talking about personal problems

**1 Circle the correct words.**

1. Oh, **no** / know!
2. I don't **think** / **know** what to do!
3. Let me **think** / **panic**.
4. What's the **matter** / **wrong**?
5. **No** / **Don't** panic.

**2 Complete the conversation with the expressions from Exercise 1.**

**Mae:** Hey, Joe. What direction are we going in?

**Joe:** ¹ _Oh, no!_ I don't believe this!

**Mae:** ² _____

**Joe:** I can't find my compass! This is terrible!

**Mae:** ³ _____ Let's think about this calmly. When did you have it last?

**Joe:** ⁴ _____ Oh, I remember. I took it out of my bag at the beginning of the hike. I must have dropped it.

**Mae:** Well, it's no big deal. We can use the sun to see what direction we're going.

**Joe:** I know, but my grandfather had given me that compass before he moved to California. It's really special. ⁵ _____

**Mae:** Oh, now I see why you're so upset. Listen, we've only been hiking for 20 minutes. Let's go back and see if we can find it.

**Joe:** That'd be great. Thanks, Mae.

# READING TO WRITE

**1  Complete Kyle's story with the adverb form of the words in parentheses.**

I'll never forget Friday, April 17. I was at my friend's house in the morning. We didn't have school that day because of high winds and heavy rain. I had heard on the news we might have a flood in our town, and ¹ _unfortunately_ (unfortunate), we did. The water was so high that our street was like a river. By noon, the rain had stopped, so my friend and I played in the street. ² _____ (natural), we thought it was fun. We didn't realize how bad things were. The water kept rising. ³ _____ (sudden), my parents showed up at my friend's house. They were really worried. They had left work early and said we had to go home ⁴ _____ (immediate). ⁵ _____ (fortunate), our house was OK, but many homes were destroyed. I felt terrible. On Saturday, I volunteered in my neighborhood to clean up the streets.

**2  Read the article in Exercise 1 again. Circle the correct answers.**

1. What happened?
   a. A hurricane destroyed many homes.
   b. There was a flood, but no homes were destroyed.
   c. There was a flood, and homes were destroyed. ⟵ (circled)

2. When did it happen?
   a. On Friday, April 17
   b. On Saturday, April 17
   c. On Saturday, April 18

3. Where was Kyle when it happened?
   a. At home
   b. At a friend's house
   c. At school

4. How did Kyle feel about the flood?
   a. At first he thought it was fun, and then he felt bad.
   b. At first he felt bad, but then he thought it was fun.
   c. At first he felt terrible, and then he got really worried.

5. What happened at the end of the story?
   a. Kyle played in the water.
   b. Kyle helped clean up the streets.
   c. Kyle's parents took him home.

**3  Complete Brianna's story with the correct sentences.**

> Fortunately, there wasn't really an avalanche.
> I was really embarrassed.
> In the end, it turned out OK.
> ✓ Last Saturday was a terrible day.
> Suddenly, my sister shouted, "Avalanche!"
> Unfortunately, I broke Tara's snowboard.

¹ *Last Saturday was a terrible day.*
I went snowboarding on a mountain near my town.
My friend Tara let me borrow her snowboard.
² _____
I got really scared, and I ran into a tree.
³ _____
My sister was joking.
⁴ _____
The snowboard hit the tree when I ran into it, and it cracked. I called Tara that night to tell her.
⁵ _____
Snowboards are expensive, and I didn't have enough money to buy her a new one.
⁶ _____
My sister felt terrible about her joke, so she gave me money to buy Tara a new board!

Unit 8 | 55

# REVIEW UNITS 7–8

**1** Write the words in the correct places in the chart.

| ✓ cement | forest fire | plants |
| compass | hurricane | rubber |
| first aid kit | metal | tsunami |
| flashlight | penknife | volcanic eruption |

| Materials | Survival essentials | Natural disasters |
|---|---|---|
| *cement* | | |
| | | |
| | | |
| | | |

**2** Look at the pictures and complete the puzzle. Find out what the city did by filling in the gray boxes.

The city _____ their trash last year by 50 percent.

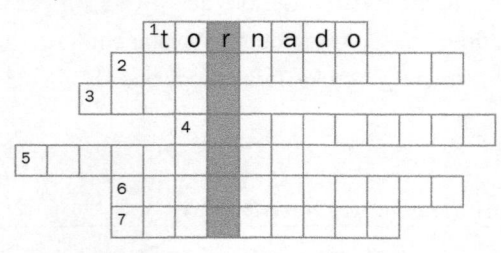

¹t o r n a d o

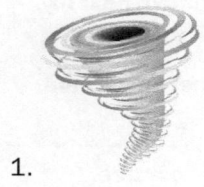

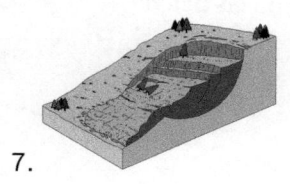

**3** Complete each sentence with a word from each box. Use the simple present passive forms of the verbs.

| build | bricks |
| design | cotton |
| make | glass |
| recycle | paper |
| turn | ✓ plastic |
| ✓ use | water |

1. *Plastic is used* to make this jewelry.

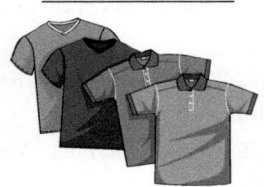

2. These shirts _____ of _____.

3. _____ bags _____ to help the environment.

4. This house _____ with _____.

5. The _____ lamps _____ by an artist.

6. The wheel _____ by _____.

56 | Review 4

**4** Put the words in the correct order to make sentences. Change the verbs to the simple past passive.

1. by / the solar panels / install / an engineer / .
   *The solar panels were installed by an engineer.*

2. the flood / save / after / our dog / .
   _____

3. build / when / the house / ?
   _____

4. not discover / right away / the forest fire / .
   _____

5. little energy / the EcoHouse / by / consume / .
   _____

6. by / invent / an American / solar panels / ?
   _____

**5** Correct the conversations. Use the past perfect.

1. A: Had you ~~hear~~ *heard* about the flood before the class?
   B: Yes, I ~~have~~ *had*.

2. A: What has you learned about Brazil before your trip?
   B: I had reading a lot about the food there.

3. A: Had Jake call you before he came over?
   B: No, he not.

4. A: Were Tom and Keiko been on a boat before their cruise?
   B: No, they haven't.

5. A: Where has you worked before you got this job?
   B: I had no worked anywhere. This is my first job.

6. A: Had you help on a volunteer project before?
   B: Yes, I hadn't.

7. A: What had happen before the flood?
   B: It has rained for several days.

8. A: Has you known about the tsunami before you went there?
   B: No, I not.

**6** Complete the article with the simple past or past perfect forms of the verbs.

Samantha and her friend Lydia ¹___*went*___ (go) on a hike last Saturday. Samantha ²_____ (not be) in a forest before the trip, but Lydia ³_____ (go) many times. Lydia ⁴_____ (tell) Samantha about the forest before they ⁵_____ (get) there. Samantha ⁶_____ (not ask) Lydia what to bring before she ⁷_____ (pack) her bag for the trip. She ⁸_____ (take) a lot of water, some snacks, and her camera. On the hike, they ⁹_____ (walk) for about an hour when Samantha ¹⁰_____ (fall) and ¹¹_____ (cut) her knee. Unfortunately, Samantha ¹²_____ (not pack) a first-aid kit before they ¹³_____ (leave) for the hike, but, fortunately, Lydia had!

**7** Complete the conversation.

| Don't panic | I didn't mean to |
| I don't know what to do | I'm really sorry |
| Let me think | ✓ What's the matter? |

**Rob:** You look terrible. ¹___*What's the matter?*___

**Ian:** I'm really worried about the hurricane.

**Rob:** ²_____. The news said it probably won't be that bad.

**Ian:** No, I don't mean the hurricane here. I'm worried about the hurricane that hit Mexico. My grandparents live there.

**Rob:** Oh, ³_____ be rude. Now I see what you mean.
⁴_____.

**Ian:** That's OK. It's just that they aren't answering their phones, and ⁵_____.

**Rob:** Do you have the number for any of their neighbors?

**Ian:** Hmm . . . ⁶_____. Yes, my cousins live close by. I'll text them now. Thanks.

# 9 He Said, She Said

## VOCABULARY  Reporting verbs

**1 Find nine more reporting verbs.**

| B | I | L | T | Z | J | O | G | V | A | Y | I | W |
|---|---|---|---|---|---|---|---|---|---|---|---|---|
| S | A | Y | P | N | B | P | R | O | M | N | S | H |
| O | N | I | S | U | G | G | E | S | T | A | T | I |
| G | N | U | W | I | S | Z | K | H | D | Y | N | S |
| G | O | U | P | U | S | T | L | O | P | G | E | P |
| E | U | F | R | Y | C | B | Q | U | A | G | M | E |
| R | N | S | O | R | H | I | L | T | R | B | A | R |
| G | C | O | M | P | L | A | I | N | E | F | N | M |
| P | E | Y | I | X | D | E | P | C | N | E | V | A |
| L | H | W | S | N | X | T | E | L | L | M | I | T |
| A | V | K | E | S | O | S | L | E | R | P | B | E |
| I | J | X | K | T | E | X | P | L | A | I | N | O |
| Y | R | E | M | I | N | D | L | A | N | N | G | P |

**2 Circle the correct words.**

1. Jennifer **said** / **reminded** she did well on her science test.
2. My dad **whispered** / **promised** me he'd drive us to the concert.
3. Who **suggested** / **announced** that we eat at this restaurant? It's great.
4. My brother always **explains** / **complains** about doing his chores.
5. Can you **promise** / **remind** me when our homework is due?
6. Diego **suggested** / **told** me about his vacation.
7. Please **whisper** / **shout** in the library. Talking loudly bothers people who are reading.
8. Lydia **told** / **explained** the computer program to us.
9. Tyrone **announced** / **said** his plans to get a summer job.
10. Maria was so surprised by a text message that she **shouted** / **told** in the middle of a store.

**3 Complete the sentences with the simple past form of some of the verbs from Exercise 1.**

1. During the game last week, the coach _____shouted_____ loudly at the players, but they couldn't hear him.
2. I _____ my best friend that I would text her when I got home.
3. My brother _____ when it was his turn to take out the trash.
4. Yesterday Kai _____ to me that we should meet after class.
5. At the assembly, the principal _____ the winner of the class prize.
6. Mr. Sato _____ the assignment to us twice, because it was a little confusing.

**4 Complete the sentences with your own information.**

1. I usually whisper _when I'm talking in the library_.
2. I often have to explain things to _____.
3. When I complain, I usually complain about _____.
4. _____ sometimes has to remind me to _____.
5. People often shout when _____.
6. One time, _____ promised me _____.

## GRAMMAR  Quoted speech vs. reported speech

**1 Add commas and quotation marks to the direct speech sentences in the correct places.**

1. Veronica said, "I was really tired yesterday."
2. I've seen that movie John announced.
3. We'll come to your party they told us.
4. Mr. Valdez shouted You can't run in the hallway!
5. Sam whispered It's dark in here.

## 2 Match the quoted speech sentences to the reported speech sentences. Use one reported speech sentence twice.

| | |
|---|---|
| 1. Maya said, "I won't call them." __d__ | a. Maya said that she called them every day. |
| 2. Maya said, "I'm calling them right now." ___ | b. Maya said that she had called them. |
| 3. Maya said, "I called them." ___ | c. Maya said that she had been calling them. |
| 4. Maya said, "I've called them." ___ | d. Maya said that she wouldn't call them. |
| 5. Maya said, "I call them every day." ___ | e. Maya said that she was calling them right now. |
| 6. Maya said, "I was calling them." ___ | |

## 3 Put the words in the correct order to make reported speech sentences.

1. was / explained / sick the day of the party / that she / Emily

   *Emily explained that she was sick the day of the party.*

2. could / me / chess / that he / Hiro / play / told

   _____

3. had / I / been / said / to Ecuador / I / that

   _____

4. was / Shelby / that she / complained / tired

   _____

5. that he / moved / Mike / had / announced /

   _____

6. said / soccer / played / that she / Alba

   _____

## 4 Complete the direct and quoted speech sentences with the correct forms of the verbs.

1. "It ___*looks*___ stormy outside," Luisa said.

   She said that it looked stormy outside.

2. "I walk my dog every day," Greg said.

   He said that he _____ his dog every day.

3. "I'll call you," Marissa told me.

   She told me that she _____ me.

4. "I _____ you," Sarah explained.

   She explained that she could help me.

5. "I _____ at the park," Nidia said.

   She said that she had been skateboarding in the park.

6. "Ling bought a new jacket," Dan said.

   He said that Ling _____ a new jacket.

## 5 Write the quotes from a website as reported speech.

1. **Katie:** I just read a great book.

   *Katie said that she had just read a great book.*

2. **Mario:** I studied all night last night.

   _____
   _____

3. **Nora:** I'll post photos of the party soon.

   _____
   _____

4. **Mia:** I can go to the soccer game on Friday!

   _____
   _____

5. **Peter:** I've lost my keys.

   _____
   _____

6. **Carol:** I'm ready for vacation.

   _____
   _____

7. **Ted:** My cousins will be in town tomorrow!

   _____
   _____

8. **Bert:** I went to a great concert on Saturday.

   _____
   _____

## VOCABULARY Communication methods

**1 Fill in the letters to complete the words.**

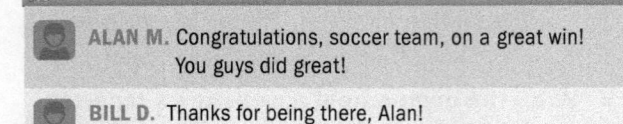

ALAN M. Congratulations, soccer team, on a great win! You guys did great!

BILL D. Thanks for being there, Alan!

1. s _o_ _c_ _i_ _a_ l _n_ e two _r_ _k_ p _o_ _s_ _t_

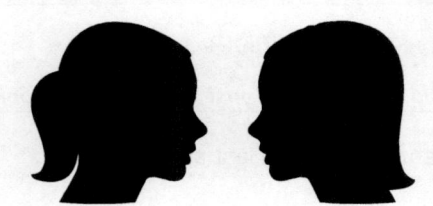

2. c _ _ _ t _ _ g

**Tonya's Recipe of the Day**
Pumpkin Cake        October 3
I know you all are going to love this recipe! It has so . . .

3. b _ _ _  _ _ _ t

4. v _ _ e _  _ h _ t

5. _ _ x _ m _ _ _ a g _

**Today's discussion:** Which apps are the best for photography?

6. f _ r _ _

7. _ h _ _ e  _ a _ l

HeartMusic04
Best concert ever! See the live video here: http://cupurl/concert

8. _ _ _ ro _ _ o _ p _ s _

From: Marci
To: Penny
Cc:
Subject: When can you go out ?

9. e _ _ i _

**2 Write the words from Exercise 1 next to their definitions.**

1. A message you put on a social networking page: _social network post_

2. Talking and seeing video of someone computer to computer: _____

3. An online discussion with several people: _____

4. Talking with others in an informal way: _____

5. A way to communicate with someone using only your voice (you can't see the other person): _____

6. A message you send to someone over the Internet that contains a subject line: _____

7. Personal writing on a website that usually shares an experience or opinion and which is usually added to often: _____

8. A short note you type on your phone and send to someone: _____

9. A very short message on a social networking page: _____

**3 Check (✓) how often you do these things.**

|   | Often | Sometimes | Never |
|---|---|---|---|
| 1. I video chat with my friends or family. |   |   |   |
| 2. I chat with friends after school. |   |   |   |
| 3. I make phone calls. |   |   |   |
| 4. I write social network posts about my day. |   |   |   |
| 5. I join online forums. |   |   |   |
| 6. I send my friends text messages. |   |   |   |

## GRAMMAR  Reported questions

**1** Match the direct questions with the reported questions.

| | |
|---|---|
| 1. "When do you eat dinner?" he asked. _d_ | a. He asked me if I had eaten dinner. |
| 2. "When did you eat dinner?" he asked. ___ | b. He asked me when I had eaten dinner. |
| 3. "When will you eat dinner?" he asked. ___ | c. He asked me when I could eat dinner. |
| 4. "When can you eat dinner?" he asked. ___ | d. He asked me when I ate dinner. |
| 5. "Did you eat dinner?" he asked. ___ | e. He asked me when I would eat dinner. |

**2** Correct the reported questions.

1. "Why are you tired?" Sandra asked.
   Sandra asked me ~~if~~ *why* I was tired.

2. Haru asked, "Who is your teacher?"
   Haru asked me who was my teacher.

3. Marcos asked, "What have you done today?"
   Marcos asked me what I have done today.

4. "Which sweater did you like?" Trisha asked.
   Trisha asked me which sweater had I liked.

5. Ahmed asked, "Can you help me?"
   Ahmed asked me when I could help him.

6. "Will you come to my party?" Anne asked.
   Anne asked me if I came to her party.

7. "Have you been online today?" asked my mom.
   My mom asked if I am been online today.

8. Dana asked, "Did you do your homework tonight?"
   Dana asked if we had been doing our homework tonight.

**3** Write the questions as reported speech.

*When can you video chat?* — Dan / Wendy

1. _Dan asked Wendy when she could video chat._

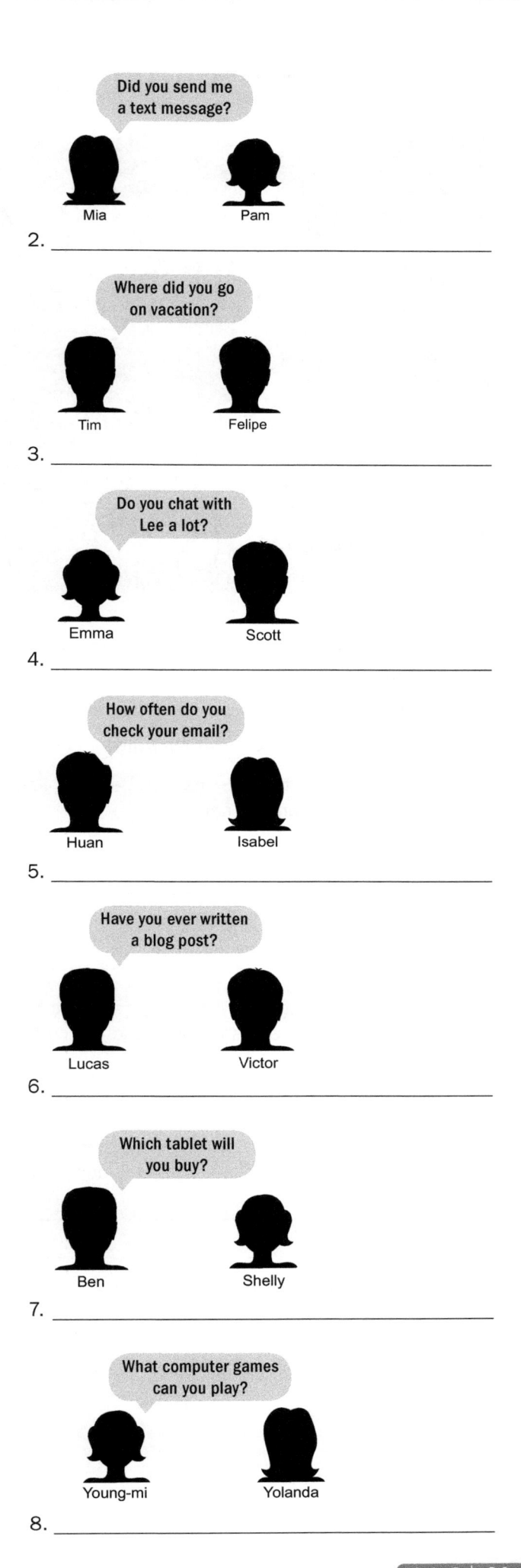

*Did you send me a text message?* — Mia / Pam

2. _____

*Where did you go on vacation?* — Tim / Felipe

3. _____

*Do you chat with Lee a lot?* — Emma / Scott

4. _____

*How often do you check your email?* — Huan / Isabel

5. _____

*Have you ever written a blog post?* — Lucas / Victor

6. _____

*Which tablet will you buy?* — Ben / Shelly

7. _____

*What computer games can you play?* — Young-mi / Yolanda

8. _____

Unit 9 | 61

## CONVERSATION — Comparing different accounts of a story

**1 Put the words in the correct order to make sentences.**

1. what / definitely / happened / that's / not / .
   *That's definitely not what happened.*

2. that Tina had cheated / had happened, / I asked Kyle / what / and he said / .
   _____
   _____

3. I / that's / what / heard / not / !
   _____
   _____

4. to detention / was assigned / Kyle / according to Jen, / .
   _____
   _____

5. with / you / how / come up / that idea / did / ?
   _____
   _____

6. had posted it / Ricardo said / online yesterday / that Kyle / well, / .
   _____
   _____

**2 Complete the conversation with the expressions from Exercise 1.**

**Lola:** We're going to have a great soccer team this year.

**Gabe:** I know. Kyle is going to be the team captain.

**Lola:** He is? ¹*How did you come up with that idea?*

**Gabe:** ² _____
His post said, "I'm so excited to be our soccer team's captain. Go Rangers!"

**Lola:** Hmm. I don't know about that.
³ _____
She said that he couldn't be captain now. He might not even be able to play on the team because he cheated on a test.

**Gabe:** ⁴ _____

**Lola:** Really? How do you know it didn't happen?

**Gabe:** ⁵ _____
She looked at his answers during the test, but he didn't do anything wrong.

**Lola:** ⁶ _____!
I heard that *he* cheated off Tina.

**Gabe:** I don't think so. Hey, here comes Tina now. Let's ask her what happened.

# READING TO WRITE

**1** Complete Leo's essay with the correct words.

For paragraph 2:

| also | in addition | ✓ for one thing |

For paragraph 3:

| first | finally | in addition |

## ONLINE RESEARCH
by Leo Rodriguez

**1** Are you like most students? Do you use the Internet for school projects and homework? Doing research online can be easy, but it can also have its share of problems.

**2** Online research is extremely convenient. ¹ *For one thing*, it can be done at school, in the library, or at home. One writer says that a benefit of online research is that the Internet is available 24 hours a day. It is ² _____ easy to find information on any topic you can imagine, simply by searching for your topic with key words. ³ _____, you can find many kinds of sources online, like newspaper and magazine articles, forums, blogs, and science reports.

**3** Although it's convenient, there can be problems with online research. ⁴ _____, anyone can post information online, and this information isn't always true. ⁵ _____, research can be dated, meaning it was posted years ago, and it may not be true anymore. ⁶ _____, some good sources, like magazines, might require you to pay to read them.

**4** I believe that doing research online is the best way to research because it's convenient and there is information available on any topic. However, I think people need to be careful. Check facts on several sites to be sure the information is true and check the dates on articles on websites. If used correctly, online research can be a great way to get information about a topic.

**2** Read the article in Exercise 1 again. Write the paragraph numbers next to each section below.

_____ A paragraph with arguments against

_____ A conclusion

_____ An introduction

_____ A paragraph with arguments in favor

**3** Read the article in Exercise 1 again. Answer the questions.

1. What does Leo use to get the reader's attention?
   _____

2. What reasons does Leo give in favor of online research?
   _____
   _____
   _____

3. What reasons does he give against online research?
   _____
   _____
   _____

4. Overall, does Leo think doing research online is a good idea or a bad one?
   _____

5. What two things does he think people can do to avoid problems with online research?
   _____
   _____

# 10 Don't Give Up!

## VOCABULARY  Goals and achievements

**1** Put the letters in the correct order to make words about goals and achievements.

1. L E D A  I H T W — *deal with*
2. K L I S L — _____
3. E A F C — _____
4. A L G O — _____
5. E D A R R W — _____
6. R S G E R P S O — _____
7. C R E M P N E F R O A — _____
8. L E H A G C E L N — _____
9. I A E H C E V — _____
10. T T C N M M I O M E — _____

**2** Circle the correct words.

1. Josh **challenged / (achieved)** his goal of running 5 kilometers in under 30 minutes.
2. How do you usually **deal with / reward** difficult problems?
3. Rita made **progress / goal** over the weekend on her school project.
4. Taking care of a pet is a **big commitment / skill**.
5. Everyone has to **achieve / face** challenges in life.
6. Playing the piano well takes **performance / skill** and practice.
7. Aimi's tennis coach **deals with / challenges** her with difficult tasks.
8. Raul's **progress / performance** at the concert was amazing.
9. The winner of the contest is **faced / rewarded** with $1,000.
10. I reached my **goal / commitment** of getting 100 percent on a math test.

**3** Complete the questions with some of the words from Exercise 1. Then circle the answers that are true for you.

1. How do you usually __*deal with*__ challenges?
   a. I face them right away.
   b. I ask friends for their opinions and then face the challenge on my own.
   c. I ask friends and family to help me face challenges.

2. How do you feel about giving a _____ in front of people?
   a. I love it!
   b. It makes me nervous, but I enjoy the challenge.
   c. I hate it!

3. Who or what do you have the biggest _____ to in your life right now?
   a. a friend or family member
   b. a pet
   c. a class or job

4. Which _____ are you best at?
   a. playing a musical instrument
   b. playing a sport
   c. using a computer program

5. Which _____ would you most like to reach?
   a. buying a house or a car
   b. getting a job
   c. finishing school

6. If you won a contest, which _____ would you most like to get?
   a. money
   b. a bicycle or car
   c. a trip to another country

## GRAMMAR  Reflexive pronouns

**1** Write the correct reflexive pronoun for each subject.

| Subject pronoun | Reflexive pronoun |
|---|---|
| 1. I | myself |
| 2. you | / yourselves |
| 3. he | |
| 4. she | |
| 5. we | |
| 6. they | |

**2** Complete the paragraphs with reflexive pronouns from Exercise 1.

### Hard Work and Rewards

When you work hard, you should reward ¹ _yourself_! Look at these examples of how people rewarded ² _____ for their hard work.

Sheila spent hours studying for a big math test. She passed the test. After the test, she went to the mall and bought ³ _____ a new phone.

Andrew trained for a 5-kilometer race. For several weeks, he only ate healthy food. After the race, he treated ⁴ _____ to a burger and French fries.

Liv and Rachel wanted to learn Spanish. Liv says, "We decided to teach ⁵ _____ Spanish instead of taking a class." They spent months learning Spanish together. As a reward, they took a trip to Mexico.

Feng wanted to learn to ski in a weekend. He went on a ski trip, took lessons, and got pretty good. He says, "I set a challenging goal for ⁶ _____, and I achieved it!" As a reward, he bought some new skis.

## Reflexive pronouns with *by*

**3** Rewrite the sentences. Add *by* and the correct reflexive pronoun.

1. My little brother can ride a bike.
   _My little brother can ride a bike by himself._

2. Can you make dinner?
   _____

3. Anna likes to travel.
   _____

4. We painted our room.
   _____

5. I learned to play the guitar.
   _____

6. Kim and Ed dealt with the problem.
   _____

**4** Answer the questions with your own information.

1. What is something you like to do by yourself?
   _I like to go to the movies by myself._

2. What is something young children usually can't do by themselves?
   _____
   _____

3. What kinds of things do you usually buy for yourself?
   _____
   _____

4. What is something that people can teach themselves?
   _____
   _____

5. What goals have you set for yourself?
   _____
   _____

6. Do you ever talk to yourself? When?
   _____
   _____

## VOCABULARY  Emotions related to accomplishments

**1** Look at the pictures and complete the crossword.

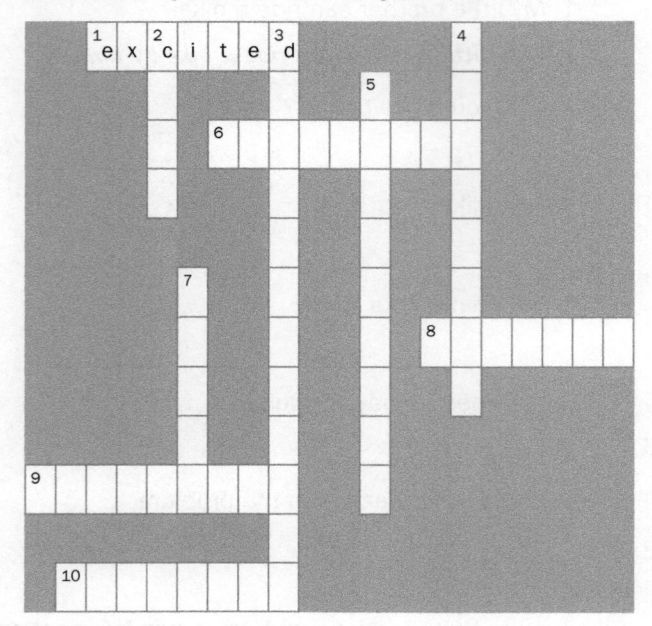

**ACROSS**
1.
6.
8.
9.
10.

**DOWN**
2.
3.
4.
5.
7.

**2** Circle the correct words.

1. My sister learned how to program computers by herself. I'm very **satisfied** / **proud** / **prepared** of her.
2. Rafael was **miserable** / **confident** / **thrilled** that his soccer team won first place.
3. Miya was **nervous** / **disappointed** / **calm** before the performance, but she did a great job.
4. I studied a lot and was **excited** / **prepared** / **proud** for the test, but it was still difficult.
5. Do you get **excited** / **miserable** / **calm** when you get rewarded for something?
6. Farah was **nervous** / **disappointed** / **satisfied** that she didn't get a part in the school play.
7. We were **thrilled** / **miserable** / **confident** on our ski trip because there wasn't any snow.
8. Are you **proud** / **prepared** / **satisfied** with your test score, or do you think you could have done better?
9. I'm **confident** / **disappointed** / **nervous** that Jenna is going to win the race. I'll be so happy for her.
10. You are always so **excited** / **calm** / **thrilled** before a presentation. Why don't you get nervous?

**3** Answer the questions with words from Exercise 1.

1. How do you feel before a test?
   *I feel nervous, but if I study, I also feel prepared!*
2. How do you feel when you achieve a goal?
   _____
   _____
3. How do you feel when you don't achieve a goal?
   _____
   _____
4. How do you feel before a trip?
   _____
   _____

## GRAMMAR  Causative *have/get*

**1  Read the sentences. Then circle the answer that correctly explains each situation.**

1. Joanna took a picture of herself.
   - a. (Joanna took her own picture.)
   - b. Another person took Joanna's picture.
2. My father has his shirts cleaned every week.
   - a. My father cleans his own shirts.
   - b. Another person cleans my father's shirts.
3. Terrance got his bicycle fixed.
   - a. Terrance fixed his own bike.
   - b. Another person fixed Terrance's bike.
4. I usually cut my hair myself.
   - a. I cut my own hair.
   - b. Another person cuts my hair.
5. Sandra gets her phone updated at TechService.
   - a. Sandra updates her phone herself.
   - b. Another person updates Sandra's phone.

**2  Correct the sentences.**

1. I ~~gotten~~ *get* my teeth cleaned twice a year.
2. We had our TV fix at Electric City.
3. Hyo's soccer team had their picture took.
4. Has Linda got her eyes checked?
5. Mr. and Mrs. Simone have had food made for Katy's party last year.
6. Carlos is getting his hair cutting.

**3  Put the words in the correct order to make sentences.**

1. her skateboard / got / last week / Lilly / fixed
   *Lilly got her skateboard fixed last week.*
2. delivered / had / we / to our mother / flowers
   _____
3. had gotten / Max / cut / for the picture / his hair
   _____
4. once a year / checked / get / my bicycle / I
   _____
5. his snowboard / painted / red and black / Jack / had
   _____

**4  Complete the sentences about what the people got or had done with the correct words. Use the simple past of *have/get*.**

| get / her car / wash | have / her eyes / check |
| ✓ get / her hair / do | have / his tablet / fix |
| get / his elbow / examine | have / their dog / clean |

1. Mary ___*got her hair done*___ yesterday.
2. Brandon _____ last week. 
3. Teresa and Leo _____ on Saturday. 
4. Linh _____ last night. 
5. Paul _____ on Monday. 
6. Janet _____ last month.

## CONVERSATION  Reassuring someone

**1 Match the phrases to make sentences.**

1. You've faced _____
2. I think I can _____
3. Try not to _____
4. I'm sure _____

a. help you.
b. you'll do fine.
c. bigger challenges than this.
d. worry about it.

**2 Complete the conversation with the expressions from Exercise 1.**

**Lucia:** Hey, Rick. How are you doing?

**Rick:** Not so good. I just fell off my skateboard.

**Lucia:** Oh, no. Do you need to have your knee checked?

**Rick:** No, it's just a small cut. I'm just worried about the skating competition tomorrow.

**Lucia:** 1 _____
You're a great skater.

**Rick:** Not worry? That's impossible! You see, I haven't been skating well lately, so I'm not feeling confident at all.

**Lucia:** 2 _____
You're probably falling because you're nervous.

**Rick:** Maybe. But I've worked so hard to achieve this goal, and now it seems impossible.

**Lucia:** Come on, Rick.
3 _____
Remember the time you competed a few months after you had broken your arm?

**Rick:** Yeah. I did pretty well in that competition. But for some reason, I wasn't nervous like I am now.

**Lucia:** 4 _____

**Rick:** Really? How?

**Lucia:** We'll skate together. We'll pretend it's the competition. Every time you fall, just get up again. We can practice all day if you want to. Before long, I don't think you'll be so nervous.

**Rick:** OK. You're right. I should keep trying. I won't give up!

## READING TO WRITE

**1** Complete the sentences with the correct words.

| achieve | addition | determined | help |
|---|---|---|---|

1. I'll need _____ from my mother.
2. In _____, I will check online to see what activities are happening in my neighborhood.
3. I am _____ to do everything by myself.
4. In order to _____ this, I will take a class about web design.

**2** Complete the text with the sentences from Exercise 1.

### Achieving My GOAL
by Denise Harris

I want to start my own blog about life in my neighborhood.
¹ _____
_____

I want to design the webpage, take and post the photos, and write all of the blog posts myself.
² _____
_____

My computer teacher, Mr. Clark, is teaching a class at the community center this summer. Then I will learn how to take better photos.
³ _____
_____

She's a great photographer. Of course, first I have to get my camera fixed. After I do those things, I'll walk around the neighborhood and take photos of things going on.
⁴ _____
_____

I'll go to as many events as I can with my camera. Then I'll write stories and post them on my blog with my pictures.

**3** Read the text again. Answer the questions.

1. What is Denise's goal?
   _____
   _____

2. What steps will Denise take to achieve her goal?
   ☑ learn about web design
   ☐ take a photography class
   ☐ have her computer fixed
   ☐ have her camera fixed
   ☐ learn to take better photos
   ☐ learn to write better in English
   ☐ take photos of activities in her neighborhood
   ☐ take photos of her life at home
   ☐ find out about activities from her mother
   ☐ find out about activities online

3. Look at the steps you checked in question 2. Which ones will Denise get help from other people to do?
   _____
   _____
   _____
   _____
   _____
   _____

# REVIEW UNITS 9–10

**1 Circle the correct words.**

1. Jana **told** / **announced** me she was nervous about her test.
2. Bob **whispered** / **shouted** loudly at the game. He was thrilled to see his brother play basketball.
3. Luis **explained** / **reminded** that he was disappointed his team lost the soccer game.
4. Jun **complained** / **said** that he was a confident speaker, so I'm sure he was calm before he gave his speech.
5. Tina **suggested** / **reminded** us that we should be prepared for the storm.
6. I was miserable about having to clean the house until Paulina **promised** / **said** to help me.

**2 Write the sentences from Exercise 1 under the correct pictures.**

1. *I was miserable about having to clean the house until* _____.
2. _____ 
3. _____ 
4. _____ 
5. _____ 
6. _____ 

**3 Cross out the word that doesn't belong to each category.**

1. **Something you type:**
   an email ~~a phone call~~
   a social network post    a blog post

2. **Something you do online:**
   video chat    send a text message
   join a forum    write a microblog post

3. **A good feeling:**
   excited    proud    miserable    satisfied

4. **A bad feeling:**
   disappointed    miserable
   nervous    confident

5. **Something people sometimes do loudly:**
   shout    announce    whisper    complain

**4 Complete the text with the correct words.**

| ✓ achieve | deal with | progress |
|---|---|---|
| challenge | face | reward |
| commitments | goals | skills |

## Ways to ¹ *Achieve* Success

- ² _____ yourself every day. Then work hard to make ³ _____ so that you can reach your ⁴ _____.
- Learn new ⁵ _____. Teach yourself or take a class to learn something new.
- Keep the ⁶ _____ you make. It's important to do the things you say you'll do.
- ⁷ _____ problems quickly. The longer you wait to fix a problem, the harder it is to ⁸ _____.
- Don't expect to get a ⁹ _____ for everything you do. Sometimes it's enough just to be successful.

## 5 Write the numbered sentences in the blog as reported speech.

### Franco's Blog

**Today's post: The future!**

Hello, friends. ¹What will you do in the future? ²Goals are important. I want to know what your goals are! ³How are you going to reach them?

**Lori:** ⁴I want to be a computer programmer. ⁵I'm taking computer classes at school.

**Aamir:** ⁶I've played soccer for 10 years. ⁷Can you guess my future career?

**Kwan:** ⁸I went to Mexico on vacation. ⁹I want to improve my Spanish!

1. Franco _asked what we would do in the future_.
2. He said that _____.
3. He _____.
4. Lori _____.
5. She _____.
6. Aamir _____.
7. He _____.
8. Kwan _____.
9. She _____.

## 6 Complete the sentences with the correct reflexive pronouns.

1. Takeko sang by _herself_ at her last music performance.
2. I'm very proud that I achieved many of my goals by _____.
3. Mindy, you shouldn't be disappointed in _____. You did your best.
4. Josh announced that he would teach _____ to speak Chinese.
5. We promised _____ that we would take a vacation next year.
6. Tim and Carla prepared _____ for a difficult task.

## 7 Write sentences with causative have/get. Use the simple past.

1. we / get / our hair / cut
   _We got our hair cut._
2. Lucia / have / her bike / fix
   _____
3. I / get / my arm / examine
   _____
4. Matt and Lynn / have / their house / paint
   _____
5. Chuck / get / his photo / take
   _____

## 8 Circle the correct words.

**Yin:** Hi, Eva. Are you ready for the music performance?

**Eva:** No, I'm not. I'm so nervous!

**Yin:** Try not to ¹**deal with** / **worry about** it. I'm sure you'll do ²**fine** / **proud**.

**Eva:** Well, I've practiced a lot, but I just don't want to go first. ³**Chatting with** / **According to** my sister, Hank Patterson went first last year, and he was so nervous that he couldn't play.

**Yin:** That's not what I ⁴**heard** / **happened**.

**Eva:** Really?

**Yin:** Yeah. I asked Hank what ⁵**had faced** / **had happened**, and he said that the audio system wasn't working.

**Eva:** I see. So, what did he do?

**Yin:** Well, Hank ⁶**said** / **told** that he didn't realize it at first. So he just played, but no one could hear him. They fixed the system, and he started again. Everything was fine.

**Eva:** I hope that doesn't happen to me. Now I'm really nervous.

**Yin:** Don't be! You've faced bigger ⁷**ideas** / **challenges** than this. You're going to be great!

# Working TOGETHER

**Unit 6 Video 6.1**

## BEFORE YOU WATCH

**1 Look at the pictures from the video. Complete the sentences with the correct words.**

| business | field | plant | together | vote | weather |

1. The prickly pear is a type of _____ that likes hot _____.
2. These women are working _____ in a _____ in Mexico.
3. The women _____ on how to run their _____.

## WHILE YOU WATCH

**2 Watch the video. Number the events 1–5 in order.**

1. The women started a business. _____
2. The cooperative sells products in the US and Mexico. _____
3. Many men moved away. _____
4. Most people worked in the fields. _____
5. The women voted on how to do things. _____

**3 Watch the video again. Circle the correct answers.**

1. What did most farms in Ayoquesco grow before 1979?
   a. prickly pear　　　b. tobacco　　　c. cactus plants
2. What happened in 1979?
   a. The factory closed.　　b. The women earned money.　　c. The farms failed.
3. Mexicans add prickly pear to _____.
   a. salads　　　b. soups　　　c. both a. and b.
4. In a cooperative, _____ runs the business.
   a. one person　　b. a small group　　c. everyone
5. In the sentence "A man from the government regularly comes to inspect their factory," to *inspect* means to _____.
   a. photograph　　b. examine　　c. visit

## AFTER YOU WATCH

**4 Work with a small group. Imagine that you're going to start a business. Discuss and vote on these questions:**

1. What kind of business will it be?
2. Where will it be located?
3. How many people are going to work there?

> We're going to start a restaurant. It will be next to the gym. About 12 people will work there.

82 | Unit 6

# Watch Your IDENTITY

**Unit 6 Video 6.3**

## BEFORE YOU WATCH

**1 Do you spend a lot of time online? Answer the questions.**

1. What personal information do you share online?
   _____
   _____

2. What information should you not share?
   _____
   _____

## WHILE YOU WATCH

**2 Watch the video. Number the sentences 1–5 in the order you hear them.**

1. Sometimes you'll get a message from someone you don't know. _____
2. A criminal just needs your name and some numbers. _____
3. You just have to be aware of who you're adding as a friend. _____
4. Social media is a great way to connect with friends. _____
5. The site will ask for your name. _____

**3 Watch the video again. Check (✓) the sentences you hear.**

1. ❑ People spend a lot of time online during the day.
2. ❑ Criminals use social media sites, too.
3. ❑ It tells you to go to a website.
4. ❑ They can use that information to get credit cards.
5. ❑ Delete these emails if you get them.

## AFTER YOU WATCH

**4 Work with a partner. Discuss: What would you do if you discovered that one of your online friends was a fake?**

> If I found out one of my friends online was a fake, I'd email him to ask who he was.

> I would delete his or her contact information from all of my social media sites.

# Where Does It ALL GO?

Unit 7 Video 7.1

## BEFORE YOU WATCH

**1 Look at the picture from the video. Answer the questions.**

What materials do you think this trash is made of?
If we throw trash on the ground, where does it go?

_____

_____

_____

## WHILE YOU WATCH

**2 Watch the video. Match the events and the places.**

1. The North Pacific Gyre is in _____.
2. There is enough plastic in the gyre to cover _____.
3. The toys fell into the sea just north of _____.
4. In 1995, some of the toys wound up in _____.
5. Between 1996 and 2000, many of the toys worked their way into _____.
6. In 2007, a few of the rubber duckies washed up in _____.

a. the Atlantic Ocean
b. Hawaii
c. South America
d. Britain
e. the Pacific Ocean
f. Texas

**3 Watch the video again. Complete the sentences with the numbers you hear.**

| ¼ (a quarter) | 29 | 71 | 139 |

1. Oceans cover _____ million square miles of Earth.
2. Water covers _____ percent of the planet.
3. People throw nearly _____ of a million kilos of garbage into the sea every day.
4. A shipment of _____ thousand toys fell into the sea.

## AFTER YOU WATCH

**4 How much garbage do you produce in a day? Complete the chart, listing everything you threw away yesterday. Share your list with a partner.**

| # | Item | Material | Where did you throw item(s) away? |
|---|------|----------|-----------------------------------|
| 2 | bottles | plastic | recycling bin |
|   |      |          |                                   |
|   |      |          |                                   |
|   |      |          |                                   |

# Build IT BETTER

**Unit 7 Video 7.3**

## BEFORE YOU WATCH

**1** Look at the pictures from the video. Complete the sentences with the correct words.

| energy | heated | roof | solar | tubes |

1. _____ from the sun is absorbed by these _____ panels.

2. The _____ on the _____ of this building contain water. The water is _____ by the sun.

## WHILE YOU WATCH

**2** Watch the video. Are the sentences true (*T*) or false (*F*)? Correct the false sentences.

1. There was a tornado in the town in 2007. _____
2. The tornado destroyed 90 percent of the homes and businesses. _____
3. The reflectors always face north. _____
4. The solar panels turn sunlight into heat. _____
5. The solar panels can power the whole building. _____

**3** Watch the video again. Circle the correct words.

1. The town was **hit / reduced** by a huge tornado.
2. It was **suggested / decided** to use solar energy.
3. How were the solar tubes **placed / put** in the roof?
4. First, holes were **drilled / made**.
5. Solar panels were **built / rebuilt**.

## AFTER YOU WATCH

**4** Work in small groups. Discuss what people in your community do to help the environment.

> Most people recycle their bottles and trash. There's a big garden downtown. People plant vegetables and flowers there.

# Land of VOLCANOES

**Unit 8 Video 8.1**

## BEFORE YOU WATCH

1 Look at the picture from the video. Complete the text with the correct words.

| active | cloud | damage | erupt | eruption | warn |

_____ volcanoes can _____ at any time. They produce a _____ of rock and ash. They can kill people and _____ airplanes. Some scientists study these volcanoes and _____ people when there is an _____.

## WHILE YOU WATCH

2 Watch the video. Answer the questions yes (Y) or no (N).

1. Is the region with volcanoes close to Moscow? _____
2. Does Sasha study active volcanoes? _____
3. Can the warning save thousands of airlines? _____
4. Did the volcano erupt a few weeks ago? _____
5. Did small eruptions continue for weeks? _____

3 Watch the video again. Match the phrases to make true sentences.

1. Sasha has visited _____
2. Sasha has taken _____
3. Their warnings can save _____
4. The seismograph had shown _____
5. Sasha and his team had to warn _____

a. activity in one of the volcanoes.
b. the airlines.
c. the volcanoes many times.
d. regular samples from the volcanoes.
e. people's lives.

## AFTER YOU WATCH

4 Work in small groups. Discuss: What natural disasters have occurred in the world in the past year? What happened?

> Last year, there was a big flood in Germany. It rained for four days. People had to leave their houses.

# Storm CHASERS

**Unit 8 Video 8.3**

## BEFORE YOU WATCH

**1** Look at the pictures from the video. Answer the questions.

1. What do you think the men are watching? Where do you think they are?
   _____
   _____

2. What natural disasters can cause this kind of damage?
   _____
   _____

## WHILE YOU WATCH

**2** Watch the video. Circle the correct answers.

1. Dixie Alley is in the _____ of the United States.
   a. north  b. south  c. west
2. The Storm Chasers are _____.
   a. teachers  b. police  c. scientists
3. _____ tornadoes are very violent.
   a. F5  b. F15  c. F50
4. The Storm Chasers try to _____ people.
   a. warn  b. talk to  c. educate

**3** Watch the video again. Complete the sentences with the correct numbers.

| 60 | 130 | 180 | 321 | 400 |

1. Every year, tornadoes kill about _____ people.
2. F5 tornadoes have winds higher than _____ kilometers per hour.
3. The F5 stayed on the ground for _____ kilometers.
4. There were over _____ tornadoes in Dixie Alley that day.
5. Unfortunately, _____ people died in the storm.

## AFTER YOU WATCH

**4** Work in small groups. Discuss: How do people get warnings about extreme weather? What do you think is the best way?

> A lot of people listen to the radio. I also check the weather on the Internet.

# Social NETWORKS

Unit 9 Video 9.1

## BEFORE YOU WATCH

**1 Answer the questions.**

1. What Internet sites do you visit most often?
   _____

2. Name two to three popular social media sites.
   _____
   _____

3. What does the number of online "friends" or "followers" someone has tell you?
   _____
   _____

## WHILE YOU WATCH

**2 Watch the video. Circle the correct answers.**

1. The narrator says that _____ changed the way people thought about video.
   a. Facebook　　　　　b. YouTube　　　　　c. Wikipedia

2. Mark Zuckerberg believes that _____ made Facebook so popular.
   a. college students　　b. high school students　　c. relationships

3. Zuckerberg explains that the *social graph* is a map of connections between _____.
   a. places　　　　　　b. people　　　　　　c. websites

4. Jimmy Wales says that communities can produce _____ of very high quality.
   a. work　　　　　　　b. writing　　　　　　c. ideas

5. All three men believe that _____ are important.
   a. schools　　　　　　b. companies　　　　　c. communities

**3 Watch the video again. Check (✓) the sentences you hear.**

1. ❏ Now, anyone with a video can be famous.
2. ❏ The Internet's about connecting individuals.
3. ❏ And, I mean, there are billions of them across the country.
4. ❏ New relationships mean new users.
5. ❏ Wikipedia is now the world's most popular encyclopedia.

## AFTER YOU WATCH

**4 Work in small groups. Discuss: What social media sites are the best for staying in touch with friends? For sharing photos? For messaging?**

> Facebook's OK for staying in touch. I use Instagram for photos, and I use my phone for messaging.

# The LANGUAGE of the FUTURE?

Unit 9 Video 9.3

## BEFORE YOU WATCH

**1  Look at the pictures from the video. Answer the questions.**

1. What language or languages do people speak in China?
   _____

2. What are some things China produces?
   _____
   _____

## WHILE YOU WATCH

**2  Watch the video. Are the sentences true (T) or false (F)? Correct the false sentences.**

1. About four billion people live in China.                                    _____
2. China has the strongest economy in the world.                               _____
3. Mandarin has over 40,000 written characters.                                _____
4. The Chinese developed a system that uses the Roman alphabet.                _____
5. The narrator asks if Mandarin is the world's number one language now.       _____

**3  Watch the video again. Complete the sentences with the words you hear.**

1. Everything in China is _____.
2. The country already produces many things, like the _____ you're wearing.
3. But everyone can understand one _____ language: Mandarin.
4. In the late _____, the Chinese developed a system called "Pinyin."
5. There are Chinese people who speak _____ all over the world.

## AFTER YOU WATCH

**4  Work with a partner. Make a list of things you own or use that are made in China. Do you think your children will speak Mandarin?**

1. backpack
2. sneakers
3. cell phone
4. computer

Unit 9 | 89

# LIFEGUARD and ATHLETE

Unit 10 Video 10.1

## BEFORE YOU WATCH

1 Look at the pictures from the video. Complete the sentences with the correct words.

| cool off | lifeguard | rescue | surfboard |

1. On hot days, people go to this beach in Australia to _____.

2. This woman is a _____. She uses her _____ to _____ people from the dangerous waters.

## WHILE YOU WATCH

2 Watch the video. Answer the questions about Candice.

1. How many people has Candice rescued? _____
2. What was her goal when she was 12? _____
3. What does she say she could not survive without? _____
4. What is her goal in the Lifesaving Championship? _____
5. How does she feel about her performance in the first race? _____

3 Watch the video again. Circle the correct words.

1. Every year, dangerous waters **take / save** the lives of people.
2. If a rescue situation **comes up / goes off**, Candice is the first one out there.
3. Sometimes she must bring people she rescues **out to shore / back to life**.
4. She must put her fears of the ocean **out of her mind / on the table**.
5. The first race is usually her worst because it takes her a bit to **cool off / warm up**.

## AFTER YOU WATCH

4 Work with a partner. What are some other life-saving jobs?

> Well, the police save people's lives, and doctors and nurses do, too.

90 | Unit 10

# Circus STAR

**Unit 10 Video 10.3**

## BEFORE YOU WATCH

**1** Look at the pictures from the video. Do you think the sentences are true (*T*) or false (*F*)?

1. In Russia, the circus is considered an art, like ballet or theater.  _____
2. The Russian government owns some of the circuses in Russia.  _____
3. Most circus acrobats perform with wild animals.  _____
4. Many Russians think that being a circus performer is an excellent job.  _____

## WHILE YOU WATCH

**2** Watch the video. Are the sentences true (*T*) or false (*F*)? Correct the false sentences.

1. Aliona dreams of being a circus director.  _____
2. Aliona's last practice doesn't go very well.  _____
3. She is performing for the top athletes in Russia's circuses.  _____
4. She earns her circus diploma.  _____
5. She decides to take her dream job in Moscow.  _____

**3** Watch the video again. Answer the questions about Aliona.

1. What must Aliona do in four weeks?  _____
2. What happens during her last practice?  _____
3. What is she offered after her performance?  _____
4. What does she decide to do?  _____

## AFTER YOU WATCH

**4** Work with a partner. Discuss: What was a goal you accomplished when you were very young? What challenges did you face?

> I really wanted to learn how to ride a bike. At first, I fell a lot, and I was a little scared of hurting myself. But now, I ride my bike everywhere!

This page intentionally left blank.

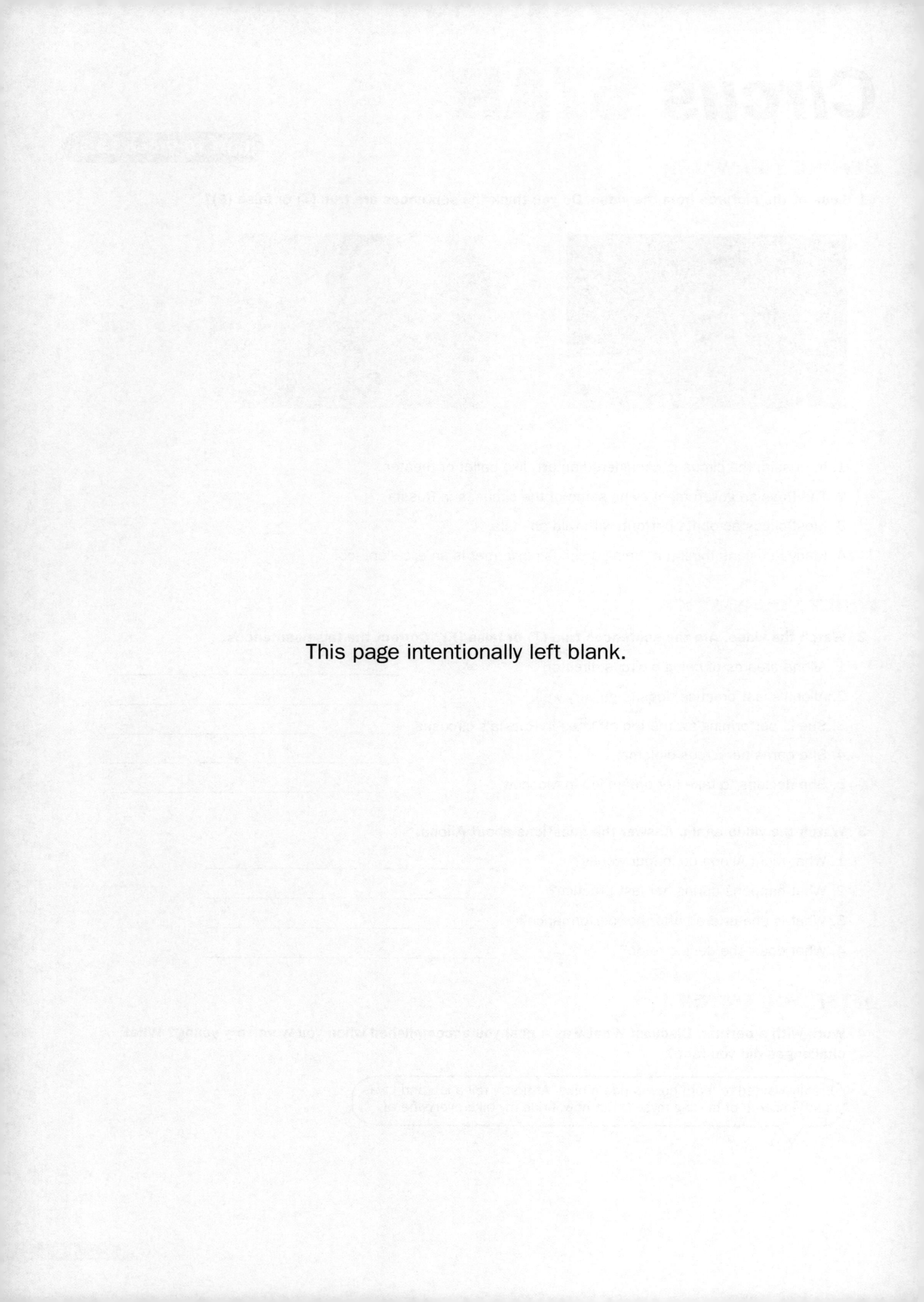

# Irregular verbs

| Base Verb | Simple Past | Past Participle |
|---|---|---|
| babysit | babysat | babysat |
| be | was, were | been |
| become | became | become |
| begin | began | begun |
| bleed | bled | bled |
| blow | blew | blown |
| break | broke | broken |
| bring | brought | brought |
| build | built | built |
| burn | burned/burnt | burned/burnt |
| buy | bought | bought |
| catch | caught | caught |
| choose | chose | chosen |
| come | came | come |
| cost | cost | cost |
| cut | cut | cut |
| deal | dealt | dealt |
| dive | dived/dove | dived |
| do | did | done |
| draw | drew | drawn |
| dream | dreamed/dreamt | dreamed/dreamt |
| drink | drank | drunk |
| drive | drove | driven |
| eat | ate | eaten |
| fall | fell | fallen |
| feel | felt | felt |
| fight | fought | fought |
| find | found | found |
| fly | flew | flown |
| forget | forgot | forgotten |
| freeze | froze | frozen |
| get | got | gotten |
| give | gave | given |
| go | went | gone |
| grow | grew | grown |
| hang | hung | hung |
| have | had | had |
| hear | heard | heard |
| hide | hid | hidden |
| hit | hit | hit |
| hold | held | held |
| hurt | hurt | hurt |
| keep | kept | kept |

| Base Verb | Simple Past | Past Participle |
|---|---|---|
| know | knew | known |
| leave | left | left |
| let | let | let |
| lie | lay | lain |
| lose | lost | lost |
| make | made | made |
| mean | meant | meant |
| meet | met | met |
| pay | paid | paid |
| put | put | put |
| read | read | read |
| ride | rode | ridden |
| ring | rang | rung |
| rise | rose | risen |
| run | ran | run |
| say | said | said |
| see | saw | seen |
| sell | sold | sold |
| send | sent | sent |
| set | set | set |
| show | showed | shown |
| shut | shut | shut |
| sing | sang | sung |
| sit | sat | sat |
| sleep | slept | slept |
| speak | spoke | spoken |
| spend | spent | spent |
| spread | spread | spread |
| stand | stood | stood |
| steal | stole | stolen |
| stick | stuck | stuck |
| swim | swam | swum |
| take | took | taken |
| teach | taught | taught |
| tell | told | told |
| think | thought | thought |
| throw | threw | thrown |
| understand | understood | understood |
| wake | woke | woken |
| wear | wore | worn |
| win | won | won |
| write | wrote | written |

# Credits

The authors and publishers acknowledge the following sources of copyright material and are grateful for the permissions granted. While every effort has been made, it has not always been possible to identify the sources of all the material used, or to trace all copyright holders. If any omissions are brought to our notice, we will be happy to include the appropriate acknowledgements on reprinting.

p. 2-3 (B/G): Shutterstock Images/John McCormick; p. 3 (a): Alamy/©Piero Cruciatti; p. 3 (b): Shutterstock Images/egd; p. 3 (c): Shutterstock Images/James BO Insogna; p. 3 (d): Alamy/©Matthew Chattle; p. 3 (e): Alamy/©blickwinkel; p. 3 (f): Shutterstock Images/Igumnova Irina; p. 3 (g): Getty Images/Sam Yeh/AFP; p. 4 (B/G): Shutterstock Images/Kathriba; p. 4 (TL): Getty Images/National Geographic; p. 4 (TR): Alamy/©RIA Novosti; p. 5 (CL): Alamy/©Jeff Schultz/Alaska Stock; p. 6 (B/G): Shutterstock Images/Yulia Glam; p. 7 (CR): Shutterstock Images/Andrey_Popov; p. 8 (L): Alamy/©Roy Johnson; p. 9 (TR): Shutterstock Images/Raymona Pooler; p. 10 (TL): Alamy/©Chris Howarth/South Atlantic; p. 10 (B/G): Shutterstock Images/Freesoulproduction; p. 11 (1): Shutterstock Images/Ashraf Jandali; p.11 (2): Shutterstock Images/Rarach; p.11 (3): Alamy/©Barry Diomede; p. 11 (4): Shutterstock Images/OHishiapply; p. 11 (5): Alamy/©EB Images/Blend Images; p. 11 (6): Alamy/©Paul Maguire; p. 12-13 (B/G): Corbis/JGI/Jamie Grill; p. 13 (a): Shutterstock Images/Syda Productions; p. 13 (b): Alamy/©Tetra Images; p. 13 (c): Alamy/©Kuttig – People; p. 13 (e): Shutterstock Images/Pressmaster; p.13 (e): Alamy/©Juice Images; p. 13 (f): Shutterstock Images/Masson; p. 13 (g): Superstock/age footstock; p. 13 (h): Getty Images/Image Source; p. 13 (i): Shutterstock Images/kuznetcov_konstantin; p. 14 (TL): Shutterstock Images/Lasse Kristensen; p. 15 (TR): Alamy/©PCN Photography; p. 16 (TR): Shutterstock Images/Lucky Business; p. 16 (a): Shutterstock Images/Ruslan Guzov; p. 16 (b): Shutterstock Images/Dragon Images; p. 16 (c): Shutterstock Images/Pressmaster; p. 16 (d): Shutterstock Images/Creatista; p. 16 (e): Shutterstock Images/Photographee.eu; p. 16 (f): Getty Images/Nick Dolding; p. 16 (g): Alamy/©Bjorn Andren/Robert Matton AB; p. 17 (TR): Shutterstock Images/Alexander Raths; p. 18 (TL): Alamy/©Kumar Sriskandan; p. 18 (BL): Corbis/Hill Street Studios/Blend Images; p. 19 (TR): Alamy/©Sverre Haugland; p. 20 (B/G): Shutterstock Images/William Perugini; p. 20 (T): Alamy/©AJSH Photograph; p. 21 (BR): Shutterstock Images/Andreasnikolas; p. 22-23 (B/G): Alamy/©JL Images; p. 23 (a): Alamy/©Jeff Gilbert; p. 23 (b): Alamy/©Michele and Tom Grimm; p. 23 (c):Alamy/©Arco Images GmbH; p. 23 (d): Alamy/©Paul Lovichi Photography; p. 23 (e): Alamy/©eddie linssen; p. 23 (f): Alamy/©Nagelestock.com; p. 23 (g): Alamy/©Tony French; p. 23 (h): Alamy/©Andrew Aitchison; p. 23 (i): Shutterestock Images/Grynold; p. 23 (j): Alamy/©Christina K; p. 24 (B/G): Shutterstock Images/Jag_cz; p. 24 (T): Alamy/©Kevin Britland; p. 25 (BL): Alamy/©LWA/Dann Tardif/Blend Images; p. 26 (TL): Alamy/©i stage; p. 26 (a): Alamy/©Aki; p. 26 (b): Shutterstock Images/Furtseff; p. 26 (c): Shutterstock Images/Vereshchagin Dmitry; p. 26 (d): Shutterestock/Christian Bertrand; p. 26 (e): Shutterstock Images/mphot; p. 26 (f): Shutterstock Images/Dario Sabljak; p. 26 (g): Shutterstock Images/Chromakey; p. 26 (h): Alamy/©lem; p. 26 (i):Shutterstock Images/vvoe; p. 26 (j): Shutterstock Images/ Visun Khankasem; p. 27 (TR): Alamy/©Graham Salter/Lebrecht Music & Arts; p. 28 (L): Shutterstock Images/Warren Goldswain; p. 29 (TL): Alamy/©david pearson; p. 30 (TR): Alamy/©ZUMA Press, Inc.; p. 30 (B/G): Shutterstock Images/Fluke samed; p. 32-33 (B/G): Getty Images/Vetta/Scott Hailstone; p. 33 (a): Alamy/©J.R.Bale; p. 33 (b): Superstock/age footstock; p. 33 (c): Getty Images/Ken Chernus/Taxi; p. 33 (d): Shutterstock Images/Greg Epperson; p. 33 (e): Alamy/©PhotoEdit; p. 33 (f): Alamy/©Age Fotostock Spain S.L.; p. 33 (g): Alamy/©Dmitry Burlakov; p. 33 (h): Shutterstock Images/PhotoSky; p. 33 (i): Alamy/©ZUMA Press, Inc.; p. 34 (TL): Alamy/©Gaspar Avila; p. 34 (BL): Alamy/©ZUMA Press, Inc.; p. 35 (CR): Getty Images/Tetra Images; p. 36 (TL): Getty Images/Philip and Karen Smith; p. 36 (BL): Alamy/©Westend61 GmbH; p. 37 (TR): Alamy/©Cultura; p. 38 (TL): Alamy/©Hemis; p. 38 (CL): Shutterstock Images/Strahil Dimitrov; p. 38 (BL): Shutterstock Images/Graphichead; p. 39 (TR): Corbis/Radius Images; p. 40 (T): Shutterstock Images/Pichugin Dmitry; p. 40 (a): Shutterstock Images/Bildagentur Zoonar GmbH; p. 40 (b): Alamy/©Howard Davies; p. 40 (c): Robert Harding Picture Library/Stuart Black/AgeFotostock; p. 40 (d): Alamy/©John Elk III; p. 40 (e): Shutterstock Images/Konrad Mostert; p. 40 (B/G): Shutterstock Images/Sasapee; p. 42-43 (B/G): Corbis/2/Andrew Bret Wallis/Ocean; p. 43 (a): Shutterstock Images/Dmitrijs Bindemanis; p. 43 (b): Shutterstock Images/Matteo photos; p. 43 (c): Alamy/©Robin Beckham/BEEPstock; p. 43 (d): Shutterstock Images/Jayakumar; p. 43 (e): Shutterstock Images/Jag_cz; p. 43 (f): Shutterstock Images/Lisa F. Young; p. 43 (g): Alamy/©Phil Degginger; p. 43 (h): Shutterstock Images/Blend Images; p. 44 (TR): Shutterstock Images/Andresr; p. 44 (1): UNIVERSAL/THE KOBAL COLLECTION/BOLAND, JASIN; p. 44 (2): UNIVERSAL/THE KOBAL COLLECTION/MOSELEY, MELISSA; p. 44 (3): HAMMER FILM PRODUCTIONS/THE KOBAL COLLECTION; p. 44 (4): MIRAMAX/THE KOBAL COLLECTION; p. 44 (5): 20TH CENTURY FOX/THE KOBAL COLLECTION/FOREMAN, RICHARD; p. 44 (6): CODE RED PRODUCTIONS/THE KOBAL COLLECTION; p. 44 (7): NEW REGENCY PICTURES/THE KOBAL COLLECTION; p. 46 (TL): Alamy/©Gunter Marx; p. 46 (BL): Alamy/©Ruby; p. 46 (BL): Alamy/©GeoStills; p. 47 (TR): Alamy/©Gunter Marx; p. 48 (B/G): Shutterstock Images/Kamira; p. 49 (TR): Shutterstock Images/Pincasso; p. 50 (TR): Alamy/©Adrian Turner; p. 50 (B/G): Shutterstock Images/Shchipkova Elena; p. 51 (TR): Shutterstock Images/Jacek Chabraszewski; p. 52-53 (B/G): Corbis/Herbert Meyrl/Westend61; p. 54-55 (B/G): Getty Images/Kevin Spreekmeester; p. 56 (TC): Shutterstock Images/Feng Yu; p. 57 (B): Alamy/©Agencja Fotograficzna Caro; p. 58 (CL): Alamy/©Denise Hager Catchlight Visual Services; p. 58 (TL): Shutterstock Images/Sean Locke Photography; p. 59 (CR): Alamy/©Richard G. Bingham II; p. 60 (TL): Shutterstock Images/IPranoffee; p. 60 (BL): Getty Images/Chris Schmidt; p. 60 (BC): Alamy/©Tony Cordoza; p. 60 (BR): Alamy/©Marjorie Kamys Cotera/Bob Daemmrich Photography; p. 61 (TL): Shutterstock Images/Ermolaev Alexander; p. 62 (B/G): Shutterstock Images/Albund; p. 62 (TL): Alamy/©Picture Partners; p. 62 (TR): Alamy/©Denise Hager Catchlight Visual Services; p. 63 (TR): Shutterstock Images/Dmitry Kalinovsky; p. 64-65 (B/G): Shutterstock Images/Albachiaraa; p. 65 (a): Shutterstock Images/Lanych; p. 65 (b): Shutterstock Images/Luchi_a; p. 65 (c): Shutterstock Images/K.Miri Photography; p. 65 (d): Shutterstock Images/Coprid; p. 65 (e): Shutterstock Images/Stockphoto Graf; p. 65 (f): Shutterstock Images/FreeBirdPhotos; p. 65 (g): Shutterstock Images/DigitalMagus; p. 65 (h): Shutterstock Images/Praisaeng; p. 65 (i): Shutterstock Images/Vadim Ratnikov; p. 65 (j): Shutterstock Images/Coprid; p. 65 (k): Shutterstock Images/John Kasawa; p. 66 (TL): Alamy/©jay goebel; p. 67 (CR): Alamy/©eye35.pix; p. 68 (TL): Alamy/©Bubbles Photolibrary; p. 69 (CR): Shutterstock Images/Minerva Studio; p. 70 (BC): Shutterstock Images/Pressmaster; p.70 (BR): Alamy/©PhotoAlto sas; p. 70 (TL): Alamy/©Jim West; p. 71 (TL): Alamy/©Purestock; p. 72 (TR): Alamy/©Justin Hannaford; p. 72 (CR): Alamy/©Chris Cooper-Smith; p. 72 (T): Shutterstock Images/CoolR; p. 72 (B): Shutterstock Images/Imagevixen; p. 73 (1): Alamy/©Cristina Fumi Photography; p. 73 (2): Shutterstock Images/Felix Rohan; p. 73 (3): Shutterstock Images/Alex Staroseltsev; p. 73 (4): Shutterstock Images/MNI; p. 73 (5): Shutterstock Images/Elena Blokhina; p. 73 (6): Shutterstock Images/Mama_mia; p. 74-75 (B/G): Corbis/Wave; p. 75 (a):Shutterstock Images/Lafoto; p. 75 (b): Shutterstock Images/st.djura; p. 75 (c): Shutterstock Images/Morten Normann Almeland; p. 75 (d): Shutterstock Images/Vaju Ariel; p. 75 (e): Shutterstock Images/Gts; p. 75 (f): Alamy/©Zacarias Pereira Da Mata; p. 75 (g): Shutterstock Images/chaoss; p. 75 (h): Shutterstock Images/jo Crebbin; p. 75 (i): Alamy/©Avico Ltd; p. 76 (T): Alamy/©Keith J Smith; p. 77 (TR): Shutterstock Images/Sekar B; p. 78 (T): Alamy/©Paul Mayall Australia; p. 78 (a): Shutterstock Images/Gresei; p. 78 (b): Shutterstock Images/Brian A Jackson; p. 78 (c): Shutterstock Images/Nikitabuida; p. 78 (d): Alamy/©BSIP SA; p. 78 (e): Shutterstock Images/Tony740607; p. 78 (f): Shutterstock Images/Grynold; p. 78 (g): Shutterstock Images/Tatiana Popova; p. 78 (h): Shutterstock Images/Ti Santi; p. 78 (i): Alamy/©D.Hurst; p. 79 (TR): Getty Images/Nacivet; p. 80 (TL): Shutterstock Images/Lamreal-kobzeva; p. 80 (CL): Shutterstock Images/scyther5; p. 80 (BL): Shutterstock Images/Ervin Monn; p. 81 (TL): Alamy/©Blend Images; p. 82 (TR): Corbis/Jim Reed/Jim Reed Photography - Severe &; p. 82 (T): Shutterstock Images/Minerva Studio; p. 82 (B/G): Shutterstock Images/Minerva Studio; p. 83 (BL): Shutterstock Images/Gorillaimages; p. 84-85 (B/G): Alamy/©Science Photo Library; p. 85 (CR): Alamy/©JGI/Jamie Grill/Blend Images; p. 86 (T): Shutterstock Images/Littleny; p. 87 (BR): Alamy/©Mark Bowden; p. 88 (a): Shutterstock Images/Syda Productions; p. 88 (b): Alamy/©Blend Images; p. 88 (c): Getty Images/Yellow Dog Productions; p. 88 (d): Getty Images/iStockphoto; p. 89 (CR): Getty Images/Debra Roets/Le Club Symphonie; p. 90 (TL): Shutterstock Images/Goodluz; p. 91 (TR): Shutterstock Images/Stephen Coburn; p. 92 (TL): Alamy/©Liquid Light; p. 92 (CL): Alamy/©Kathy deWitt; p. 92 (BL): Alamy/©Tim Graham; p. 92 (B): Shutterstock Images/FrameAngel; p. 94-95 (B/G): Corbis/Pete Saloutos/Image Source; p. 96 (TL): Shutterstock Images/Arieliona; p. 97 (TR): Alamy/©Redsnapper; p. 98 (TL): Alamy/©Steve Lindridge; p. 99 (CR): Alamy/©Paul/F1online Digitale Bildagentur GmbH; p. 100 (TL): Alamy/©Robert Harding World Imagery; p. 100 (BL): Alamy/©Bob Daemmrich; p. 101 (TL): Alamy/©Steve Skjold; p. 102 (T, B/G): Alamy/©Zuma Press; p. 104-105 (B/G): Corbis/Marc Dozier; p. 120 (BR): Alamy/©The Print Collector; Back cover: Shutterstock Images/fluke samed.

Front cover photography by Alamy/©Martin Strmiska.

**The publishers are grateful to the following illustrators:**
Q2A Media Services, Inc. p. 6, 116, 120; Martin Sanders p. 28.

**All video stills by kind permission of:**
Discovery Communications, LLC 2015: p. 2 (1, 3, 4), 5, 10, 11, 12 (1, 3), 15, 20, 22 (1, 3, 4), 25, 30, 31, 32 (1, 3), 35, 40, 42 (1, 3, 4), 45, 50, 51, 54 (1, 3), 57, 62, 64 (1, 3, 4), 67, 72, 73, 74 (1, 3), 77, 82, 84 (1, 3, 4), 87, 92, 93, 94 (1, 3), 97, 102, 116, 117, 118, 119, 120; Cambridge University Press: p. 2 (2), 8, 12 (2), 18, 22 (2), 28, 32 (2), 38, 42 (2), 48, 54 (2), 60, 64 (2), 70, 74 (2), 80, 84 (2), 90, 94 (2), 100.

# Credits

The authors and publishers acknowledge the following sources of copyright material and are grateful for the permissions granted. While every effort has been made, it has not always been possible to identify the sources of all the material used, or to trace all copyright holders. If any omissions are brought to our notice, we will be happy to include the appropriate acknowledgements on reprinting.

p. 2 (1): Shutterstock Images/Michael Wick; p. 2 (2): Shutterstock Images/Menno Schaefer; p. 2 (3): Shutterstock Images/Ragnisphoto; p. 10 (CR): Alamy/©Tetra Images; p. 21 (TL): Alamy/©Juice Images; p. 25 (TL): Alamy/©Keith Morris; p. 27 (TR): Getty Images/Manfred Rutz; p. 28 (BR): Alamy/©Maria Galan; p. 38 (CL): Getty images/Roy Mehta; p. 44 (1): Alamy/©Ruslan Kudrin; p. 44 (2): Shutterstock Images/Elena Elisseeva; p. 44 (3): Shutterstock Images/Gtstudio; p. 44 (4): Shutterstock Images/Quang Ho; p. 44 (5): Shutterstock Images/Sophie McAulay; p. 44 (6): Shutterstock Images/Coolkengzz; p. 44 (7): Alamy/©Paul Debois; p. 44 (8): Shutterstock Images/Yevgeniy11; p. 49 (TR): Shutterstock Images/Mila Supinskaya; p. 55 (TL): Alamy/©Acumen images; Back cover: Shutterstock Images Images/Fluke Samed.

Front cover photograph by Alamy/©Martin Strmiska.

**The publishers are grateful to the following illustrators:**
Janet Allinger p. 6, 8, 34, 40, 68; David Belmonte p. 4, 16, 17, 42, 43, 70; Galia Bernstein p. 18 (BR), 20, 23, 45, 46; Anni Betts p. 5, 37, 39, 66; Nigel Dobbyn p. 12, 26, 30, 33, 50, 54, 62; Mark Duffin p. 18 (1-10), 52; Q2A Media Services, Inc. p. 9, 11, 28, 50 (1, 2, 4, 5, 9), 56, 60, 61, 76; Jose Rubio p. 14, 31, 47, 48, 67.

**All video stills by kind permission of Discovery Communications, LLC 2015.**

# Notes

**Notes**

# Notes